Awesome
Altars

Awesome Altars

How to Transform Worship Space

Mary Dark

AND

Judy Pace Christie

Abingdon Press
Nashville, Tennessee

AWESOME ALTARS: HOW TO TRANSFORM WORSHIP SPACE

Copyright © 2005 by Mary Dark and Judy Pace Christie

This book is printed on acid-free recycled paper.

Library of Congress, Cataloguing in Publication Data

Dark, Mary.
  Awesome altars : how to transform worship space / Mary Dark and Judy Pace Christie.—1st ed.
    p. cm.
  ISBN 0-687-33181-1 (alk. paper)
  1. Altar guilds. I. Christie, Judy Pace, 1956- II. Title.

  BV195.D37 2005
  247'.1—dc22
                    2005016181

Scripture quotations noted NIV are taken from the HOLY BIBLE, NEW INTERNATIONAL VERSION®. Copyright© 1973, 1978, 1984 by International Bible Society. Used by permission of Zondervan Publishing House. All rights reserved.

Scripture quotations noted NRSV are taken from the New Revised Standard Version of the Bible, copyright 1989 by the Division of Christian Education of the National Council of the Churches of Christ in the United States of America. Used by permission. All rights reserved.

Scripture quotations noted TNIV are taken from Holy Bible, Today's New International Version ™ TNIV® Copyright© 2001, 2005 by International Bible Society®. All rights reserved worldwide.

ISBN 13: 978-0-687-33181-9

08 09 10 11 12 13 14 — 10 09 08 07 06 05 04 03 02

MANUFACTURED IN THE UNITED STATES OF AMERICA

With Appreciation

The development of a new approach to altar design and the organization of Tribes of Dan owe their life to so many. Without the divine help of God and earthly assistance from scores of people, this book and DVD could never have been produced.

We offer special thanks to Dr. Rob Weber, senior pastor of Grace Community United Methodist Church in Shreveport, Louisiana, and Stacy Hood, director of Worship Ministries at Grace, for their leadership, friendship, and openness to innovation in worship. Their encouragement to explore new ways to grow as followers of Christ has enriched both of our lives enormously.

We also thank the faithful Tribe of Dan members who serve so creatively week after week. They are the heroes of this story. We appreciate so much the people from a variety of churches who shared their stories with us. Huge thanks go to Phyllis, Beth, Karen, Sandy, Rebecca, Patti, Patty and Patty (yes, all three Patties!), John, Scott, Bryan and Joel for help with the DVD and photographs, from gathering materials to camera work to cleaning up, and to Alisa and Pat for editing help and encouragement.

Thank you to Mary's family members, Don, JoAnne and Huel Jones, for their inspiration and the use of so many items for altars through the years.

Finally, we thank the rest of our patient and loving families—including Tom, Leah and Allen Dark and Paul Christie. Thank goodness for husbands who cook! We are in debt to Allen, who directed the DVD efforts and went above and beyond again and again to make this project better, always an adventure, working between his mom and Judy.

About the Cover

May the words of my mouth and the meditation of my heart be pleasing in your sight,
O Lord, my Rock and my Redeemer. Psalm 19:14 (NIV)

The Bible repeatedly uses the word "rock" to describe God's strength. We love using rocks for altar design. The "Rock of Ages" altar on the cover was inspired by a rock garden at a regional park. The cross is made from used roof slate, purchased from an area dealer, and is constructed using L-brackets. The cross is enhanced with beautiful flowers. Patty McAllister, a member of the Tribe of Dan at Grace Community United Methodist Church, designed this altar, creating something beautiful out of a messy process. We enjoy using non-traditional items like roofing material to draw in worshipers. We hope you will find, as we have, that rocks are great items to use in altar design. We have even accumulated a rock pile near the back door of our church! One warning, however: This cross is quite heavy and difficult to move. You will need lots of help or will need to construct it near the altar space at your church. You can read more about this altar in chapter 9. The photograph was taken by Sean Gregory.

Then the LORD said to Moses,
"See, I have chosen Bezalel
son of Uri, the son of Hur, of the tribe of Judah,
and I have filled him with the Spirit of God,
with skill, ability and knowledge in all kinds of crafts—

to make artistic designs for working gold, silver and bronze,
to cut and set stones,
to work in wood, and
to engage in all kinds of craftsmanship.

Moreover, I have appointed Oholiab son of Ahisamach,
of the tribe of Dan, to help him. Also I have given skill to all the
craftsmen to make everything
I have commanded you."

Exodus 31:1-6 NIV

In memory of
Mary's mother,
Leah Evans Jones,
who started it all by making her daughter
get up early on Sunday mornings
to take flowers to church

Contents

Using the *Awesome Altars* DVD

Welcome to *Awesome Altars*—an illustrated tool kit that will provide you with inspiration and ideas for how to integrate altar design into the worship experience, transforming worship space into an atmosphere that honors God and helps people to worship more fully!

The *Awesome Altars* DVD, located at the back of this book, provides further information about and instruction on altar design. The DVD consists of the following parts:

- **Eleven video segments:**

    Section 1: Crosses

    Section 2: Candles

    Section 3: Plants

    Section 4: Props

    Section 5: Containers

    Section 6: Fabric & Colors

    Section 7: Tools & Storage

    Section 8: Tabletop

    Section 9: Drama & Wedding

    Section 10: Advent

    Section 11: Basic Arrangement

- **Altar Examples** (a color slideshow of the eighteen altars featured in chapter 9 of the book)

- **Calendar** (a color slideshow of the liturgical calendar)

- **Worksheets** (Word document versions of several of the book's worksheets that can be modified to suit your own specific needs; there is also a Word document of the liturgical calendar that can be modified to suit your own specific needs.)

- **Credits**

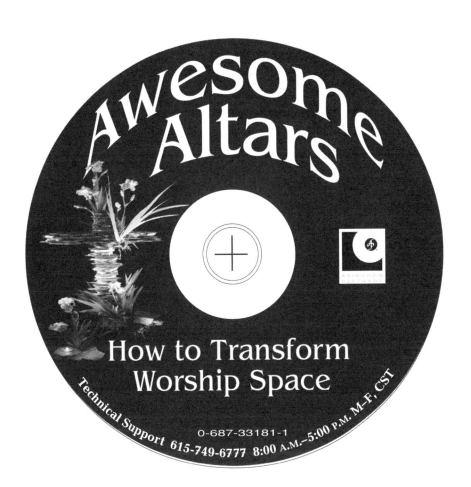

Playing the DVD on a Set-top Player

Set-top DVD players are connected to a TV. If you have previously played a DVD motion picture, you will see that the *Awesome Altars* DVD behaves in the same way. Once inserted, the disk will begin playing automatically and will first bring up the copyright screen, followed by an introduction. After the introduction, the Main menu will appear. You may choose to skip over the introduction by highlighting SKIP THIS OPENING and pressing Enter. This will take you directly to the main menu.

To navigate through the DVD menus, use the Up and Down arrow keys on your remote to move the pointer to the menu item that you wish to view. After an item is highlighted, press Play to move to the next screen, to begin playing one of the video segments, or to advance a slide in a slideshow. The slideshows are not set to automatically advance. You must advance them manually, one screen at a time, by using the Play button on your DVD remote control. Clicking the Title button will take you back to the very beginning of the disk.

Volume is adjusted in the normal way for your DVD player. Other buttons on the remote, like Fast Forward, will allow you to quickly move through a video or jump to the next item on the screen.

Many of the screens have embedded graphic buttons, such as Main Menu, to help you navigate. Selecting the graphic Main Menu button will always take you to the main menu. You can also use the Menu button on your DVD remote control to take you to the main menu. (You will note that the main menu and the video menu are two separate menus.)

Using the DVD on a Computer

If you have the capability to hook a computer with a DVD player to a projector, you may choose to use this method to display the video segments and the slideshows. Every computer will have a different type of proprietary software that comes with the DVD drive, and the controls on each will vary slightly. Many of the buttons on the software interface will act just like the buttons on a DVD remote, though there will be some variation. Using the Up and Down arrow buttons on your software remote will cycle through highlighting each of the buttons, functioning just as they do on a set-top DVD player. (Up and Left will move through the buttons clockwise; Down and Right will move through the buttons counter-clockwise.) Once you have highlighted the button you want, hit the Enter key to activate the button. The advantage, however, of the computer navigation over the DVD set-top player is your ability to use the mouse to easily select the item you want by clicking on it.

In general, clicking the Menu button will take you back one step: if you are simply in a menu, it will take you up one level to the previous one; if you are playing a video, it will stop the video and take you back to the section sub-menu. You can also use the Menu button to exit a video or slideshow. Depending on where you are, you may have several choices when you click the Menu button: Title will take you back to the very beginning; Root will take you to the section sub-menu.

Clicking the Title button will take you to the back to the very beginning of the disk. The Fast Forward and Rewind buttons will allow you to advance or rewind the video. Next and Previous will only work to advance you through the slides in the slideshows.

How Do I Access the Worksheets on the DVD?

Worksheet templates from the book as well as a liturgical calendar have been included on the DVD for use with your altar design team. These files are included as Microsoft Word documents and can be found in the Worksheets folder on the DVD. To access the original files for these resources, you will need to insert the disk in your computer DVD drive. Browse to the file listing by using Windows Explorer (PC) or by double-clicking the DVD icon (Macintosh). Double-click the Worksheets folder. Then select the file you want, and either copy the file to your hard drive or double-click the file name to open it from the disk.

Join Us and Help Draw People to God

A few years ago, a terrible ice storm hit our community at Christmastime. Special flowers and foliage ordered for our church altar were grounded in a city several hours away. Approximately ten minutes after we got that news, a church member called, upset. "You don't know me," he said, but went on to explain that a thirty-year-old tree that he and his wife had planted had been broken by the heavy ice. "Is there any way it could be used on the altar?" he asked.

A team of church members carefully traveled to his home to discover a gorgeous holly tree covered in red berries, resting on the ground. The resulting altar design was prettier—and more meaningful—than the one originally planned. That beautiful natural collection of materials, donated with such feeling, contributed to an awesome altar. God's hand was obvious in how the altar came together, and the altar itself was connected organically to the experience of the community.

During another church service the altar was covered with antique baskets and well-worn wooden boxes overflowing with fruit and vegetables: squash, apples, potatoes, pears, a pumpkin, beets, and green beans. A plain wooden cross rose from their midst, and a single candle burned. As the pastor preached about the importance of giving our first fruits to God, he turned to the altar, picked up a squash, and held it for illustration. The altar enhanced the sermon and provided a beautiful backdrop for worship. It was an example of integrating altar design into the entire worship service, an emerging concept that combines traditional ideas with innovation and creativity.

This book and DVD are offered to help you learn how to develop an altar ministry at your church, to show you how this approach can help people more fully worship God each week and help individuals grow in their faith. This approach has been dynamic in our church and in the lives of those we train. The Holy Spirit moves in awesome ways through altar design—in people who are touched by the beautiful work in worship each week and in those who use their God-given talents to put together altars.

As our world changes continuously, churches struggle to adapt to these changes while maintaining the traditions and biblical foundation upon which they were built. In Matthew 9, Jesus talks about putting new wine into old wineskins. "Neither do people pour new wine into old wineskins. If they do, the skins will burst, the wine will run out and the wineskins will be ruined. No, they pour new wine into new wineskins, and both are preserved" (Matthew 9:17 TNIV). *Awesome Altars* is also about new wine and new wineskins. Imaginative, resourceful, and worshipful ideas come together to create altars that are full of meaning and add variety to the worship experience. Along the way, individual lives are changed, and you will begin to hear story after story about how altar ministry deeply affects people.

Perhaps your church has contemporary services where you look for new ways to present the old story. Or perhaps you attend a more traditional church where you are searching for new ideas to express ageless themes and concepts. This book and accompanying DVD can help make the altar an integral, God-honoring part of the worship service. You can develop a team of people who want to use their unique gifts to serve God—whether as a carpenter building a prop, an artist weaving cloth, a gardener growing or arranging flowers, or a volunteer who simply likes to help prepare the church for worship.

This material will help you cultivate ideas and handle practical matters such as assembling a toolbox, dealing with critics, and finding storage space. We will offer you eighteen altars you can try at your church — including altars for the special seasons of Advent, Easter, and Pentecost. In addition, we will walk you through a practice session. We will also teach you how to start a biblically-centered small group to serve in this ministry.

Our group is called the "Tribe of Dan," but you should call yours by a name that works for your church and your group. We encourage you to find a name that has meaning and can keep you focused on your mission. "Tribe of Dan" comes from the book of Exodus, and we are happy for you to use it, too, if you want. Or perhaps another Bible passage will speak to you and lead to a new name. For example, one congregation in Nashville, Tennessee, refers to its altar-design team as "Lydia's Friends." Lydia was a worshiper of God who made a living as a dealer in purple cloth. Her conversion and the house church that she apparently began are described in Acts 16.

By any meaningful name, your group can learn to enhance the worship spaces at your church, and your "Tribe" members will have the opportunity to grow together as disciples.

The Tribe of Dan ministry uses altar design to enhance worship, and it has evolved during the past several years at Grace Community United Methodist Church in Shreveport, Louisiana, where the two authors are members.

One week early in the church's life— the week before Mary's first visit to the church—Pastor Rob Weber mentioned that people were welcome to bring flowers from their yards for the bare altar. As Mary slipped into her seat that first Sunday, she quickly noticed that there were no flowers on the altar. However, moments before the service started, a child walked up to Rob and handed him a small Styrofoam cup with one pansy in it. He took the tiny flower and placed it reverently on the altar, as though the small petals were the most beautiful arrangement he had ever seen. That moment struck Mary with a great force. It reminded her of the widow's mite story in the Bible, where the woman gave all she had, even though it was a small amount.

As a retail florist for thirty years, Mary had designed flowers for nearly every church in town, including many big churches with big budgets. She was touched deeply by the pastor's appreciation for this little cup with one pansy. As the service continued, she was moved further by the sermon—a message about the importance of using our hands and feet and the gifts God gives us for the Lord's service. That spoke strongly to Mary about the gift of flowers. She realized that she had flowers left over in her floral shop each week, so why not offer these to the church?

As the weeks unfolded, an odd thing happened in this Southern flower shop. Mary began to notice that the most beautiful flowers that arrived in her shipments each week were the ones that suddenly did not sell. Thus, they were the ones left for the altar. A powerful lesson from the Scriptures took root when Mary slowly began to know that each of us owes God our best and most beautiful, not merely the leftovers.

From that realization, the altar design ministry developed even more, and other people began to get involved. Tribe of Dan classes were organized, and we began to see the impact of awesome altars in other churches. More and more props were used. Altars became unique and more significant.

Judy came to the church a few years later, when the ministry was up and running. One of her first impressions of a new church home was the striking altars and how inspirational they were each week—filled sometimes with big, bold, and unusual flowers and at other times with blooms you might normally find in your grandmother's yard or by the side of the road. Interesting items full of symbolism surrounded the flowers and greenery. Each week the attention to detail for the altar and the way it complemented the sermon and music was incredibly moving. Altar-design ministry was one of the many things that drew Judy to the church because it reinforced how important worship is for this church. Here the worship of God is taken seriously—while overflowing with joy. Many elements were put together. Obvious thought and planning, with a spiritual attitude, went into each service.

As the months passed, Judy began to inquire about the altars and sought out Mary to tell her how moving the altars were. While attending a statewide spiritual leadership academy, Judy gingerly helped design a handful of altars for a series of retreats, growing from Mary's guidance and comments. "This is not that hard," was Mary's consistent message. "You can do it. Just listen for God's direction."

We are happy to share with you our experiences, with Mary's help as the teacher and Judy's help as the person sitting in the pew, appreciating and questioning. We will tell you of the many joys and bumps along the way; what we have learned, and what we would do differently. We will even tell you about times when things did not go the way we thought they might. Occasionally that has resulted in a much more awesome altar than we had hoped. At other times, we confess, it has resulted in a misstep—such as the time that a Tribe member thought the altar theme was "yolk" instead of "yoke." (More on that later!)

We hope that these experiences at many churches can help you encounter a new ministry opportunity and help you enjoy worship even more. We have observed altar design evolve from a static and at times stuffy process to something that is relaxed, fun, and deeply spiritual.

Altars should be as unique and special as you and your church. The Tribe of Dan is a ministry not limited to one church. It can flourish at your church and open new ways to worship and to hear from God. You can use your talents and the guidance of the Holy Spirit to create awesome altars that draw people to God. Along the way, may you discover, as we did, that you are blossoming in your faith and learning new things as a follower of Christ.

CHAPTER ONE
A Meaningful Purpose

Come, let us bow down in worship,
  let us kneel before the LORD our Maker;
  for he is our God and we are the people
    of his pasture, the flock under his care.
            Psalm 95:6-7 (TNIV)

Following a Sunday morning service at our church, a mother approached the front of the sanctuary, crying. The altar was covered with an abundance of orangey-red spider lilies, profuse and beautiful. The woman was expecting a visit that day from her daughter, with whom she had had a difficult time. Spider lilies were her daughter's favorite flower. The altar helped the mother begin to move further toward reconciliation with her child. She left to meet her daughter, carrying flowers given to her from the altar.

After another service, a woman called the church office to request a photograph of a very natural altar design, one covered with a reed screen and many shades of brown. The cross was made of wooden reeds. She told the person answering the phone that the Holy Spirit had spoken to her during the sermon, adding to her worship through the altar design.

The use of altar design to enhance the worship experience visually can be remarkably powerful and can open another path to hear God's voice during worship. Altars are not awesome because they look great or are extremely creative (although that is an acceptable side benefit). Altars become awesome when the Holy Spirit uses this ministry to speak to those who put together the altars and to those who view the altars in worship.

Innovative and creative altar design can draw individuals nearer to God by:

- Helping the congregation focus on what is being spoken

- Connecting what the minister and music are saying

- Planting a visual image to carry throughout the week

- Moving far beyond basic flower arrangements that change little from week to week

The altar connects with the overall worship experience and helps build a sense of continuity and community. It says immediately that something special is going to happen and that the place is full of energy and impact drawn from God's presence. Beautiful altar designs remind us of God's creation—the beauty of flowers, greenery, rocks, and other natural materials. They call us to worship with candles and crosses and other sacred pieces. The altar offers a picture postcard for the mind to enjoy repeatedly during the week.

Stacy Hood, Director of Worship Ministries for our congregation, observes that the altar is viewed as a window to the Holy One, making a divine connection. "Altar design has the same presence as music and preaching…These items happen every week. We don't always have a drama, a dance, enhanced multimedia, or other added layers of connection. However, the altar design team provides a level of multisensory connection that is used every week. People often come up after worship to take a closer look at the altar. It provides a deeper entry into the message and experience of worship."

This attention to worship spaces is not new. It is part of the tradition of worship outlined in the Old Testament. In Exodus 31, God commands that the tabernacle space should be filled with "artistic designs" (NRSV). God chose people with certain talents, individuals such as Bezalel and Oholiab, who were filled "with the Spirit of God, with skill, ability, and knowledge in all kinds of crafts" (NIV). Among these leaders were members of the tribe of Dan who were "to help." These were the people chosen to roll up their sleeves and get the work done. With permission and authority, they became the leaders for design. Their leadership was necessary to carry out divine commandments that were given to Moses.

While cultures have come and gone, and artistic or architectural styles have evolved through the centuries, there can be no doubt that a congregation requires imaginative people with skill and ability to transform worship space into an environment that glorifies God and invites God into our hearts and minds. After considering this rich biblical example, is it any wonder that imagining the altar and other components of our sacred space is part of the way we worship God?

Serve as needed, listening to the Holy Spirit

The commandment to Moses also reminds us that we are called to help design and symbolize the ideas of others, which means we willingly serve as needed to make the worship environment more meaningful. Sometimes an artist can have a strong ego and may be tempted to ignore the images and guidance from others. However, worship design is based on teamwork. This means that the altar artist is always thinking from the outside-in and does not try to impose his or her ego on seekers and believers. The artist who listens will avoid this temptation and will take into account the input of the team. **This service to the congregation requires rolling up your sleeves and listening to the Holy Spirit.**

The Tribe of Dan altar design group at our church was born after studying Exodus 31 in a small group. The text describes this form of service before Moses came down the mountain with the Ten Commandments. In Exodus 30:1-6, the people were given a detailed description of the altar and how it was to look. Creating the worship space was given a high profile. We sense this same type of divine leadership in the development of the Tribe of Dan. Through altar experiences, God speaks time and again, and our worship is taken deeper in so many ways.

One week early in the movement toward a new approach to altar design, Mary had a strong sense that she was supposed to do something different. Feeling a bit sheepish, she imagined that the item she was to use was in her bedroom. She took a pair of old blue jeans, which were sticking out from under the closet door, cut them up, and wrapped them around a cross that was already at the church. Other pieces of denim were placed in vases with wild flowers.

As people entered the church that day, they seemed a bit baffled over the use of jeans but also expressed how much they enjoyed the different altar. During the service, the pastor picked up one of the vases and asked the congregation, "Do you know what this means?" Mary's immediate thought was: "Thank goodness. Now *I'll* find out what this altar is about!" The minister went on to say that this was the last week for him to remind people to bring blue jeans to be donated to missions. An eighteen-wheeler would be collecting them for a national drive to give clothing to people in need. "I was supposed to remind you last week," he said.

Between services, Mary explained to the pastor that she had no conscious idea to use the blue jeans for that purpose, but that she had felt a strong urge to use them. She and the pastor looked at each other and said, "I think we're onto something here."

Many congregations are grappling with the challenge of change in their worship services, while remaining committed to upholding the sacred truths of God's love and mercy. They want to weave new ideas and patterns into traditional ways of doing things. Inventive altar design, created by those committed to the work of the church, can help.

Who is the Tribe of Dan today?

The Tribe of Dan could be called an Altar Guild because it builds upon the traditions of such guilds. The Guild has traditionally consisted of a group of people, usually women, who are responsible for care of the altar. Their duties ordinarily include making certain that the altar cloth, cross, and candles are in place and helping to assemble items needed for the Lord's Supper. Often the Guild is also responsible for making sure that flowers are provided for the altar, including arrangements given in memory or honor of individuals.

In other ways, however, the Tribe is very different from the conventional idea of an Altar Guild. The Tribe is careful not to discard significant traditions and practices, but seeks to move visual ideas to a different plane of imagination. The standard flower arrangement in worship services is replaced with a design that relates to that day's sermon and music. A cross and candles are still placed on the altar each weekend, but there is not an *exact* or *correct* structure of altar design. Tribe members are encouraged to allow the Holy Spirit to guide them in creatively interpreting the message of the service.

The members of the Tribe are people who come together each week to help create a church's altar (and potentially the entire worship environment). These are people who want to use their gifts, whether they are listening for the voice of God for inspiration and direction, or using a particular skill or knowledge of crafts to make worship more full and fresh.

Tribe members may be carpenters, quilt sewers, or painters—including those who can paint a wall or a piece of furniture as well as those who can use a brush to create images on canvas. They may be those with good organizational skills such as telephoning and scheduling, craftspeople of all kinds, and other enthusiastic people who want to contribute their talents to visual ministries. They often are individuals who prefer to serve in the background, rather than out front teaching a class or making a speech.

As well as for people who want to serve behind the scenes, the Tribe of Dan and altar design can open up service areas for all sorts of people who may not even believe they have a talent. You will notice again and again how this ministry draws into service new people who might not have participated in any type of church program before. As churches start this ministry, they offer strong and nearly instant feedback on how it begins to pull people in. One Tribe of Dan organizer in another town describes the assimilation in this way: "[Altar-design ministry] is an excellent way to get participation from the congregation because we need crafters, sewers, wood people, gofers, shoppers, organizers—and ideas."

As willing workers begin to design new altars, people in the church begin to come forward to donate items for use, which is similar to how the book of Exodus describes the furnishing of the tabernacle. Church after church that has embarked upon this approach to altars tells of the unexpected offerings of flowers, greenery, wood, or many other items that draw attention to the altar. People who contribute supplies are also members of your altar tribe.

While making a list of the types of people who serve, we recall the names of a great host of Tribe mates. We could rattle off quite a long list of real people! We know also that the same types of everyday folks will come forward to serve and help as *your* altar-design ministry develops. People will be moved by God to make a difference in your church. *As your list of artisans develops, you will be astonished at the wonderful individuals who will come together to serve, pulling out gifts you might never have imagined needing, much less actually finding.*

In the book of Exodus, those who were working on the sanctuary "left their work and said to Moses, 'The people are bringing more than enough for doing the work the LORD commanded to be done'" (Exodus 36:4-5 NIV). Moses actually had to tell them not to bring more "because what they already had was more than enough to do all the work" (Exodus 36:7 NIV). Most pastors would relish this sort of problem. We have witnessed the same kind of capacity or abundance problem in our congregation and in many others. Remarkably, this joy spills over into many of our other church ministries.

Transforming worship

Altar creators develop a significant ministry that combines a variety of gifts and hands-on talents with worship. This ministry can add a new dimension to a worship service and can even help *transform* worship. Ideas you already have and routines you already follow can go to a new and highly integrated level with a fresh approach to altar design. The servants move beyond the rote "order the altar arrangement" way of thinking to developing a customized design that honors God and leads others into worship.

An altar volunteer at a Catholic church describes the influence like this: "The first thing people see when they come into our church is the altar. That moment of impact should say, 'Welcome to the celebration of God's word.' The people need to feel that they are a part of a community, that the Mass is a celebration, and that what we have put up draws them into the liturgy. The church environment is very important to a worship service. The symbols, flowers, banners, drapes, and arches all say, 'This is a special occasion—a moment of celebration and rejoicing as community in prayer and liturgy.'"

Pastor Rob Weber says, "The use of visual elements on the altar allows people to experience the message and the act of worship on a variety of levels. Sometimes the images and objects present on the altar serve as a backdrop for a song or the sermon. At other times the altar becomes part of the message itself."

Glenda, a busy and faithful member of a nearby church, offers strong testimony to this idea from the perspective of one who began by observing from the congregation. She got involved in altar design at the request of her pastor, who had seen it move many participants at a clergy gathering. "Doing altar design has taught me many things." Glenda observes, "Visuals are all around us, but connecting the altar with a Bible verse makes the sermon more meaningful… introducing the altar design to our worship service helped in so many ways. It was an attention-getter from the start. We concentrated more on the pastor's sermon because we were trying to figure out the connection between the altar and the sermon. Understanding the connection got to be fun."

When you are open to the Spirit of God, as were the people in Exodus 31, you will be amazed at how altars and worship opportunities unfold and how your church will be blessed. Stories will begin to emerge time and again with examples of how God works through altar design and visual worship. To get this ministry under way, start small. Share the simple things of nature and materials that are easily available. Tell the stories of what is symbolized on the altar. Help people make the connection. Before long, worshipers will look to the imagery on the altar as a part of the multifaceted experience of the presence and message of God.

Worksheet: Getting Started

1. Why are we considering altar ministry at our church?

2. How can this ministry help our church with its vision and purpose?

3. Are we ready to roll up our sleeves and work, while listening to the Holy Spirit?

To pray about: How an altar-design ministry can bring people in our church closer to God and deepen their worship.

Notes:

CHAPTER TWO
Customizing this Ministry for Your Church

Be shepherds of the church of God,
which he bought with his own blood.
Acts 20:28 (TNIV)

In a tiny country sanctuary in North Louisiana, a church member cuts beautiful flowers from her yard and places them lovingly on the altar and piano. She is happy to share with her fellow worshipers these incredibly lovely heirloom blooms, the flowers an unusual color that she especially likes. Her immense joy at providing these flowers is shared by the early arrivers at church this morning, as they talk about the color and the arrangement and her gift to the church.

A short drive away, a mother, daughter, and grandmother laugh and visit as they work around the altar at their large, urban church, a job they do with great enthusiasm several times a year. They prayerfully examine the sermon topic, Scripture, and stories the minister might use. They have been led to search for unique greenery and different sorts of crosses and candles to highlight their efforts. They use a variety of interesting props.

The altar-design ministry at your church should be customized to your church and will unfold over time, just as your church tweaks and assesses and adjusts programs and approaches over the years.

Words of advice:

- Anything you do with your altar ministry must be subject to prayer from the beginning.

- It is not necessary, nor practical, that you overhaul your entire process at once.

The fact-finding process

As you contemplate starting (or changing) the altar-design ministry at your church, put on your reporter's hat for some basic fact-finding. You will need to:

1. Assess how your church is currently handling the altar each week and how the approach might change.
2. Talk to a variety of people to explain your ideas and why you want to enact them.
3. Listen to concerns and potential problems in shifting the way the altar looks.
4. Gently respond to criticism that may come from the thought of something new.
5. Saturate your efforts in prayer.
6. Be prepared to explain that new approaches to altar design are another tool to help people worship God and retain more of what they hear in the service. (In the same way that a song may thrill someone's heart and reinforce the message of the day or a video clip may help someone understand a tough part of the sermon, so can the altar help people understand the point the service is trying to get across.)

Each person is created differently and learns and worships in different ways. By taking a new approach with altars, the altar design process can help broaden the reach or impact of the service.

Consider the five Ws: who, what, when, where, and why

- **Who** needs to be involved in your process and informed of your ideas?

- **What** steps do you need to take to make this work?

- **When** is a good time to try a step in this new direction?

- **Where** will the group meet, and where will you store your materials? Will your designs go on the altar, in the foyer, or elsewhere in the church?

- **Why** should you consider a change?

The first "who" to get involved is, of course, God. You must pray for God's guidance in using you, for support from key people, for creative ideas, and for the Holy Spirit to permeate your work. *Without a strong commitment to and reliance on God, this integration of a visual approach into worship will not work.* Never forget, even as your altar ministry matures, to pray for God's guidance.

Once you have prayed about becoming more creative with the altar, it is time to approach the leaders of the church. For us, the creation of awesome altars—and the organization of our own Tribe of Dan—began following a brief letter to the senior pastor, expressing a willingness to donate some flowers to the church and to adorn the altar. As the ministry developed, conversations followed. As your ministry grows, you may want to assign one person to serve as the liaison with the pastor. (It is important not to overwhelm a busy pastor with three or four people calling to go over the same details.)

Creating different altars, keyed to the sermon and music of worship services, needs the approval and support of the church's key worship leaders. As mentioned in the book of Exodus, the design of worship space is part of an overall plan for worship and should not become a renegade unit.

Banish the idea that you are actually keeping the pastor or worship director in the loop; they *are* the loop. Your visual ideas and designs should spring from their plans for the content of the overall worship experience. If you have a worship leader or coordinator at your church, that person must be consulted and must become part of the process. Communicating with and following instructions from this person can help your Tribe live within its biblical mandate to be helpers and to make sure that the work of assembling the altar gets done.

If you have an active Altar Guild at your church, its members must also be part of this discussion. You cannot simply waltz in one day and announce your plans to change the way the altar looks. You will need to work within this group, and the pastor can help you with the integration.

One of the challenges of developing a Tribe of Dan is to blend old ways with new ideas. This can be stressful and painful if not handled in a prayerful and deliberate way. For example, if a Guild or class has for decades provided a pink carnation for each new baby girl born, you may want to suggest new ways to present the pink carnation. You do not want to announce one day that you will no longer use the carnations, perhaps unintentionally sending a message that the gift is not appreciated or that the birth of the child is not recognized. An option might be to have a place in the entryway or vestibule of your church where such traditions are expanded, honoring births, anniversaries, and other occasions. Or perhaps you begin to invite people to donate money for altar design supplies and plants, rather than ordering traditional arrangements.

You might want to pull together a group of church leaders to discuss ways that the church is changing and how the visual component of worship can best work with these changes. These people—from an administrative council to the choir—might offer ideas on how the altar can look different and be a stronger part of the service. Be sure to ask for support, input, and approval of the concept. The involvement of each of these people can prevent your new ministry from withering before it has a chance to develop.

As you discuss altar design with your worship leaders and others in your church, you need to be asking specific questions. The answers to these questions will help shape your altar tribe and focus your efforts.

Once you have discussed the concept of new altar design with key leaders, it is time to decide *who* **else might be involved in this challenge.**

Perhaps the members of a traditional Altar Guild will want to help, or perhaps you know of someone in the church who has a creative talent that could be useful. Along the way, there is no doubt that God will send people to help with this work.

Implementing the altar-design ministry also requires knowledge about whom you need to involve in your particular church. To whom do you answer as you implement designs? From whom do you need to get information? (In most churches it will be the worship leader or pastor.) Who is in charge of the worship space for the worship service? (This could be fragmented: choir director, pianist, minister, or Altar Guild.)

Who makes the decisions in your church, particularly about building design? If you want the area behind your altar painted (as we did), whom do you ask? (On the DVD, you will see our "problem" wall behind the altar.) If you want to implement what some might consider a drastic change, who must give the OK?

The next step is to consider *what* **small steps you might take to get started and** *what* **else you need to know.**

Look for a way to connect the dots between a particular service's music and sermon, or between a sermon series and the church events. The altar can help pull together individual pieces. This integration is at the core of what you are trying to do.

You will also need to answer other questions that are more specific:

1. Does your congregation use a lectionary? The Revised Common Lectionary is a three-year cycle of several hundred passages from the Bible, used by more than twenty

denominations. Some denominations (Anglican and Roman Catholic) use a two-year lectionary. It is designed to encourage the public reading of Scripture, which offers continuity in preaching themes and broad coverage of texts from the Old and New Testament. Will the lectionary be your source for Scripture reading, if not for sermon preparation? (See *The Revised Common Lectionary: The Consultation on Common Texts*, 1992 (ISBN 0687361745). Or visit http://www.commontexts.org/ and http://www.gbod.org/worship/lectionary for more information on the lectionary.)

2. Are paraments used? (Paraments are usually fabrics that cover the altar table or pulpit or lectern. They are often symbolic, with various images, whether draped or hung.)

3. Does your ordained minister wear a robe and stole? If so, you will need to coordinate those with the altar design and colors of the Christian year. (More information on the colors of the Christian year is given in chapter 5.)

4. What are the rules in your church? Can the altar be completely covered, moved, or changed in any way? Who made the rules? Are they negotiable? Can you start slowly so that over time the rules become more negotiable?

One group who embarked upon this new approach to altars in its neighborhood Catholic church offers the following advice to a church or individual who is beginning altar-design ministry: "Find out the dos and don'ts of your denomination, the wishes of the priest or pastor, and who is doing what in the church. You must be sure that you are not stepping on anyone's toes. Sometimes you

must coordinate with other people. There are many people in this invisible ministry, and you must dig them out."

Decide *when* you will start—whether with a weekly altar-design meeting where you pray and come up with ideas or during a meeting with the worship team.

You might consider an introductory meeting with potential team members to solicit volunteers and to explain how creative altar design can help different people worship God in a new way.

You must also decide when you want your first work to appear. Perhaps you want to start with the altar on a special occasion or season, such as Advent, when churches traditionally have many activities converging in the worship space.

Choose *where* the group will meet, *where* you will store materials, and *where* you will create your designs.

You will need to arrange a location for group meetings as well as a location for storing altar-design materials. For convenience, you may want to see if there is space available at your church.

You will also need to consider where you will display your first design. You might want to begin with the altar, or you might want to take a different approach. If your church is resistant to change, or if the traditional space for worship is a static symbol of the congregation's heritage, you might consider starting in the foyer area, perhaps on a round table. This can help people become familiar with new, visual pieces of worship. As this develops, you might ask the person making announcements or even the pastor in his or her sermon to mention the foyer design as it relates to that day's message. Explanations or interpretations of the altar can also be mentioned in the bulletin to help people learn about new ideas.

Perhaps the most important of the Ws is *why*. Creating special altars for each week's service is intended for one core purpose: to help people more fully worship God.

Changes in how churches do things, including worship space, can often be difficult. Some people will likely ask why change is needed at all. Others may see this as reinventing the wheel, or change for the sake of change. Perhaps a candlestick or cross is the memorial gift from another generation, many decades in the past, but is still protected by inherited leadership positions on the church board(s). Some reluctant person might suggest that the church does not need "decoration." While these reasons or constraints are real and may require compromise, you must help others see that any approach to altar design is intended to help a church better serve God and to lead people into a meaningful experience with Jesus Christ. The altar must always remind us that Jesus is the reason for our worship, the place where we remember and commune with the risen Lord.

Sometimes it is helpful to recall that church worship and traditional rituals have been changing for centuries. Rarely does any church—including yours—stay the same. Change in altar design can be helpful in drawing new worshipers to the message of Christ, injecting new energy into an old sanctuary, and planting new seeds in the lives of veteran members.

Help participants and those throughout the church understand that using the altar more effectively in worship is a simple way churches can approach change. The altar will still include the cross and a candle, but perhaps not a brass cross and two white candles. It will include worshipful components that take traditional ideas and infuse them with new ways of seeing things.

Remember to pray!

As you raise a variety of questions and seek answers within your church community, remember to seek answers from God all along the way. Prayer is vital as you put together altars, altar teams, and an altar ministry. Prayer reduces competition, binding us together as we visualize God's grace.

Worksheet: Customizing This Ministry

1. How has our church changed over the years? What have we learned from these changes that can be useful as we consider an altar-design ministry?

2. How does this ministry help with worship and small-group efforts at our church?

3. With whom do I need to talk about possibilities for our altar-design ministry?

To pray about: Wisdom, patience, and love in trying a new approach.

Notes:

CHAPTER THREE
Building a Terrific Team

There are different kinds of gifts, but the
same Spirit distributes them.
There are different kinds of service, but the
same Lord.

1 Corinthians 12:4-5 (TNIV)

Sandy had always wanted to help create the altar, but her church did not have a group that did such work. So when she moved to Louisiana from West Virginia, she chose a church where she could be part of altar-design ministry. She has become a key part of the Tribe of Dan. Sandy is quick to say she is not the most artistic of the group, but her fellow volunteers know she offers a gift they could not do without—the gift of organization. She helps set up meetings, pull together details, and get everyone on the altar-design schedule. For the use of these skills, the Tribe regularly says "thank you" to God! In return, Sandy's altar work has helped her in two ways. It has taken her mind off some of her physical problems, and it has offered a small group to love and care for her.

Annie is a vibrant woman who has used her creativity in the arts community for many years. She is excited as she tells about her experience with altar design. "Doing the altar is one of my greatest joys. I use the saris and shawls that my friend has brought me from all over the world. I made a cross this summer with my dad. The wood came from a beloved dogwood tree that had to be cut down at his church in Maryland. For me, those items that come to our altar from far away illustrate the point that we are not just a congregation in Shreveport, Louisiana, but a part of the whole body of Christ all over the world!"

Our worship director loves the Saturday morning each year when the entire altar ministry comes together to prepare the church for Advent, and everyone on the team is invited. Describing last year's perparations, she says:

I was reminded again of one of the many reasons I am so amazed by this ministry area. People were buzzing around everywhere, hauling in materials, hanging objects from the ceiling in the gathering area, and preparing the altar. As I looked across the worship area, I saw Miss Loma sitting on a bar stool by the altar. She was helping another team member pin little pleats in the cloth that would go all the way around the altar. No one would ever see those pleats, since they would be covered by greenery, but those pleats affected the way the material hung, and it was amazing to see how that invisible detail was key to the altar imagery.

Miss Loma wasn't on a tall ladder or hauling in materials, since she is in her eighties and moves a little slower than some…and with much more grace than many ever will. Yet she is a valuable member of the altar ministry. She has a wonderful eye for God's beauty through the visual arts, and her spirit brings a great depth to the team. There is always an important role for her to play when she participates.

Another altar design team member who serves in countless ways is Patty. During a recent church conference, we placed hundreds of unplanted bulbs on tables and on the altar, symbolizing what is still to come and that God has put within us all that we need to go forth. Patty helped keep the bulbs separate, knowing they would be planted for later use on an altar. She also contributed other bulbs that she had recently received. After the conference, she used her knowledge of plants to figure out when the bulbs should be planted to bloom for use at Easter. We absolutely relish her beautiful collection of gifts that she freely gives to those who worship.

Each of these people illustrates how altar design draws together individuals to use unique gifts in service to God. They are classic examples of how each person is gifted in different ways and can serve in unique ways. And they remind us that the right people seem to show up when there is a need.

Growing disciples through service

The idea for an altar-design team is not limited to a certain kind of church with a certain approach to worship. It is already in place in most congregations. Each week, people come together to prepare the altars in churches everywhere. As they ready candles, crosses, flowers and other materials, they are following an ancient tradition intended to help others more fully worship God. They are serving God by adding a visual component to worship and adorning God's house.

One of the responsibilities of the church is to help grow and develop disciples for Christ. The altar-design ministry helps grow and develop disciples by:

- Seeking people who are looking for a place to serve

- Bringing together small groups of people to work toward a common goal

- Helping members better know one another

- Helping people learn to recognize and develop their unique gifts, often opening them up to other areas of service and stewardship

The altar-design ministry does each of these things in the name of Christ—with a focus on worship and as an act of stewardship of time and talents.

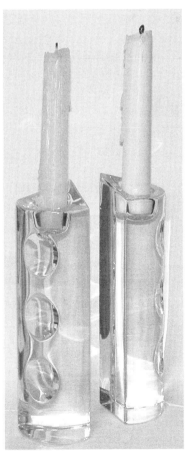

Members of altar-design groups often are not the usual people who have been involved in ministry at a church, perhaps not the Sunday school teachers or committee leaders. They often are people who have been searching for their place and have had a hard time finding it. Some have an artistic side and feel as though they do not fit into traditional ministry areas. They believe that they do not have anything to offer or that their talents are not worth much. Many people think they have no talent at all.

One of the exciting things about developing an altar design team is that the members will likely be unlikely!

A boy's gift to the church

Your ministry will touch people in ways you cannot even begin to imagine. Consider, for example, one of our favorite design experiences, which involved the sweet gift of a young boy. This ten-year-old child was at a local store with his mother and saw some candlesticks. "Mama, come here and look," he said. "I want to buy these for the altar at church." His mother was surprised and caught off guard.

In a gentle way, she tried to dissuade her son. "Those are pretty," she said, "but I can't afford them." Her son, who had never been involved in altar design in any way, was not to be discouraged. He told her he wanted to buy them with his money, and they went home to get it.

His mother, bemused by the experience, contacted the Tribe of Dan and said her son had bought candlesticks for the altar. She wondered what she might do with them. The Tribe invited him to bring them to church on Saturday morning to help with the altar design.

He arrived that Saturday morning with a young buddy, both dressed in uniforms to head straight to a ballgame after their work at church. With help, they put the pretty blue glass candlesticks, a precious gift from this boy, on the altar. Then they were assigned the job of filling vases with water and arranging blue hydrangeas near the altar. "Huh?" they asked, a bit surprised. They had not realized that they could be part of the altar design in ways that went far beyond the candlestick donation. As they created, they had a great time. The boy's friend said, "We could never do this at our church. I can't wait to tell my Mom that I got to help with the altar today." When they finished, one of the boys' big brothers came to get them in his pickup truck. They climbed in and headed off to their ballgame, full of life and ready for a new adventure— the unlikeliest new members of the Tribe that we had ever seen!

How do you identify team members?

Creating beautiful altars is not some magic talent that only one person can possess. Instead, it is a team effort that uses the different skills of different people. Remember Sandy, the organizer; Annie, the creative person; and the ten-year-old ball-playing designer?

- First, as with each offering of your work, pray. Ask God to help you discern those who might be looking for a place to get involved but have not yet found one.

- Next, think of people you know who might be helpful— an artist who is always creating something distinctive, a hard-working volunteer who is dependable and shows up with a smile, a church member who frequently compliments special efforts you make with the altar or foyer design.

- Ask church staff members if they have recommendations. They may know someone who has gone through a spiritual gifts class, for example, and is looking for the right place to serve. Or they may have a list of people who have expressed an interest in worship ministries. Because the Holy Spirit is involved in shaping lives in churches, sometimes a chance encounter with a staff member will help plug just the right person into the altar design team.

- Don't overlook friends who might have interests similar to yours and who could be quite good at developing and arranging altars.

- The tried-and-true notice in the bulletin almost always draws participants and gives everyone a chance to sign up. (You can also post this on your church Web site.) This technique works well when we recruit for our Tribe. The message usually reads something like this: "Don't think you have a creative bone in your body? Let God prove you wrong!" It then lists details on how to get information on the Tribe of Dan.

From one church came this report: "We have acquired a list of parishioners with information they filled out concerning their talents and interests such as gardening, flowers, sewing, carpentry, arts, and crafts. There is also a new survey soon to be sent that should enlarge our search. One day we hope to pull them all together in a Tribe."

Developing and training members

After you draw up a list of likely volunteers, you will probably want to pair them with existing altar-design team members to provide information and listen to ideas. Another approach is to invite new volunteers to a get-acquainted meeting and talk with them about their ideas on altar design at your church. Many people are busy and may not want to add another meeting to their lives, so the one-on-one tactic may work better.

Whatever approach you take, make sure you provide potential volunteers with adequate information and that you listen to them. Be open to possibilities here. Do not try to lead them into your preconceived idea of how the process might work without getting their feedback.

During your first meeting or during this conversation, you might share your vision for this creative team and tell them the story of the design of the tabernacle in Exodus 31. Or, you may want to read together the words from Romans 12:4-8:

For just as each of us has one body with many members and these members do not all have the same function, so in Christ we, though many, form one body, and each member belongs to all the others. We have different gifts, according to the grace given to each of us. If your gift is prophesying, then prophesy in accordance with your faith; if it is serving, then serve; if it is teaching, then teach; if it is to encourage, then give encouragement; if it is giving, then give generously; if it is to lead, do it diligently; if it is to show mercy, do it cheerfully. (TNIV)

Brainstorm with the group about how different people in the church serve, and ask for thoughts about how certain gifts can help enhance the worship experience and the joyful design of altars.

Ask for a commitment to serve

After this meeting, it is time for participants to sign on the dotted line and to commit to help with this ministry on a regular basis. That commitment doesn't mean that each person must be there for every service. The calendar and planning take into consideration scheduling issues such as vacations and work. At the end of this chapter, you will find a sample commitment worksheet. You may simply copy this form and ask each member to sign it, or you may use it as a guide to create your own form. The form is intended to help with reliability and show the importance of this work. It also makes it clear that Tribe members are expected to roll up their sleeves and work, preventing the occasional problem you will encounter with people who want to be Tribe members in name only.

The fun of developing the skills of volunteers

You have the opportunity to train and guide your team. The coach of any team must make sure the right players are in the right places and must plug people into the part of the process that is right for them. Some will be of more help in brainstorming and tying altar ideas together with the theme of a service. Some will enjoy gathering materials, while others will want to do the actual work of putting the pieces together on the altar. Still others may wish to serve by removing materials after a service and putting them away.

When pulling together a team, consider scheduling organized training that focuses on goals for the group. As we heard from one altar ministry volunteer, do not assume that just because someone has a gift for this that they know how to do it. "Gifted is not necessarily educated. There are principles that provide a path to follow or a navigation tool to help find our personal way of expression."

One way to generate discussion and help identify how the process can work is to list descriptive words for awesome altars that aid worship. Then, discuss what might be used on altars that are *inspiring, peaceful, exuberant,* etc. What might an inspiring altar look like? A peaceful altar? An exuberant altar?

You can also choose a Bible verse or story and ask Tribe members to think of how they might illustrate the text on an altar. Consider Galatians 5:22-23: "But the fruit of the Spirit is love, joy, peace, patience, kindness, goodness, faithfulness, gentleness and self-control. Against such things there is no law" (TNIV). What sort of altar could visually explain these words? Would this be an altar covered with real fruit? Or might there be a variety of baskets with the word "love, joy, peace, patience" and so forth painted on them and fruit coming out of the baskets?

Another passage that is good for practice and training is Psalm 25:4-5: "Show me your ways, LORD; teach me your paths. Guide me in your truth and teach me, for you are God my Savior, and my hope is in you all day long" (TNIV). What ideas does your group have for illustrating this text on the altar? What props and materials might you use? Could you use a classroom theme, or maps? One altar design might include a piece of board painted with chalkboard paint, with words written on it.

Have fun coming up with ideas, and let imagination run wild. Remember that a key part of this experience is to teach people to think differently. There really is no wrong approach at this point.

As the group is organized, look for leaders who will be responsible each week for the altar design. **Week in and week out, you will need someone who is in charge of making sure the altar is ready to go.** That person will help lead the group in prayer about design and implementation and will have ideas that will help shape the initial concept.

How altar-design meetings generally work

The entire altar-design team might meet together only twice a year, and those can be working meetings. As you work, discuss what is coming up next and bounce ideas off each other. This is also a great time for team members to get acquainted and observe who works well together. You can also talk about problems that might have arisen in recent months, such as a member who is relocating or how to make altars more interactive. Your meetings might serve as a time for you to remind each other of the ways in which specific altars have touched people's lives. You might also laugh about some of the mistakes that you have made!

Some of *our* mistakes include forgetting to clarify who would add water to a fountain we were using on the altar—too many people added water, and the fountain overflowed. We noticed the problem just before the service was to start, resulting in a quick visit to the front of the church with a mop. Another time, the sermon was about building, and we had made a cross out of different building materials and tools by using Velcro to bind them to the surface of the cross. That worked great until the items all let go at the same moment. We're grateful that the items fell at a perfect moment in the sermon, when the pastor talked about things falling apart!

Other team meetings can be more informal, made up of people who are working together on a particular altar or people who through the Tribe become friends who encourage each other. Another meeting approach suggested by an altar-design volunteer is to meet as a small group at least twice a month, exploring and cultivating gifts with fellowship, study, and hands-on projects.

An altar design representative can participate at meetings of the larger worship team. At our church this is the SPIN team, which helps develop worship services. SPIN is a group organized for **S**haring Ideas, **P**rojecting into the future and **I**magining on **N**eutral ground, through the leadership of the worship director. The Tribe of Dan is an integral part of SPIN. "Many people have a hard time understanding how it is that so many elements come together for worship," says the worship director. "From altar design to musicians, we place an emphasis on flexibility. It is about doing what is best for the big picture of worship."

While the ultimate goal of worship is to experience God, we must realize that people experience God in different ways. One person may be touched by communion or the sermon or a song or by the warmth of a greeter's welcome. In the same way, a creative altar might move another. As Pastor Rob says, "Having visual imagery on the altar allows visually oriented people to connect with the message and the worship experience at a different level. In a visual culture, especially among postmoderns, multiple layers of aesthetic interpretation and information presentation are very important." Karen, an altar ministry volunteer, observes: "I love how the altars can bring to life the sermon. I think that an altar designer who has studied the Scripture and prayed about a vision for the altar can really help 'interpret' the message that is to be delivered."

The purpose of SPIN is to bring together all elements into a cohesive message for each service. The group is made up of those who have a part in leading worship—including the worship leader and representatives from other areas such as hospitality, drama, and visual ministries. The pastor may or may not attend but is kept informed. The SPIN team works to expand the variety of worship experiences, with altar design as a part of the process.

Through all of this, a bond is formed, which results in enhanced worship and effective community. In one instance, for example, the husband of a Tribe member was in a terrible car accident that left him in the intensive care unit for weeks. He had helped Tribe members make one of our favorite crosses, covered in smooth, black river stones. After his accident, Tribe members took him one of the stones from that cross—"his" cross. That rock was allowed in the ICU and became a source of strength during an excruciating recovery.

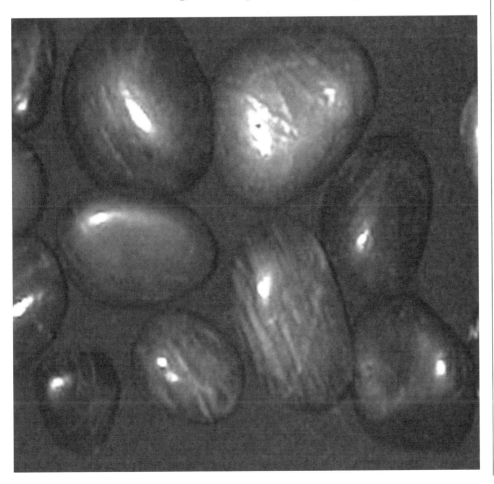

Worksheet: Sample Commitment Form

As you join the _____ (insert name of team), we ask that you be a member of this church or worship at this church regularly. We believe that in order to serve as effectively as possible, you need an understanding of the practices and beliefs of this church. We encourage you to participate in classes to learn more about the church and to grow spiritually.

Designing creative and worshipful altars each week requires a commitment of time and energy. Our team members rotate these responsibilities, and you will be asked to help on a regular basis. As a team member, you will need to come to church ahead of time to assemble the altar design. You may also be called upon to make changes or freshen the altar for other services.

We ask that you be an active part of our team of brothers and sisters in Christ, growing together and helping each other as a church family. You will be asked to work as a team with the worship leader and pastor, understanding that they have the final say in this church's altar designs.

We welcome you into the _____ (insert name of team)!

MY COMMITMENT TO THE _____ MINISTRY:

I understand that my participation in the _____ ministry requires a commitment of time and energy. I understand that this involvement is a ministry and will offer me a chance to grow and to help others grow too. I commit to be a member of the team and to help this church community as it seeks to worship God more fully and to grow closer to Christ.

_____

Signature

_____

Date

CHAPTER FOUR
The Altar Table and Worship Environment

Worship God!
    Revelation 22:9*b* (NRSV)

If you attended worship services as a child, you probably recall the type of altar your church had. And you may believe this is the "right" kind of altar.

When the two of us were girls, we both attended Baptist churches—one a small rural church and the other an inner-city neighborhood church. While different in some ways, both of these churches had many things in common, including the altar table.

Each church had a table that was small, rectangular, and semiformal. We grew up believing that altar tables are *supposed* to look like this.

When entering the church we now attend, one of the first things you might notice is the altar table that we use most of the time. This table is quite different from the altar tables of our youth. Made of cypress, it is an old, eleven-foot-long informal table. This beautiful altar was originally a table in a general store. Antique lovers would probably call it primitive in style. It works terrifically as an altar.

The type of table your church uses is one of the many traditions that define worship. Many congregations still use

the smaller, more formal tables. While table style can change the approach to altar design, it does not prevent you from creating unique, inspirational altars. This ministry can truly be used for any size altar; the activities of the altar ministry are meant to be customized for your church culture, by staying alert to what works well in the physical environment.

Various branches on the Christian tree have different requirements for how the altar is adorned. Roman Catholics, for example, have prescribed practices to follow, such as using only a white cloth on the top of the altar and letting nothing obstruct the line of sight to the altar.

In addition to considerations about the altar table, worship spaces come in many sizes and shapes. Tradition can meet innovation in the worship environment, whether it is a contemporary multiuse room or a more formal cathedral. One church might have a basilica design with a rectangular building, a broad nave ending in a semicircle with a domed roof, and colonnaded aisles. Another might have the half-round or theater architectural style. Some churches have a center aisle. Others have aisles to the left and right of a center section. Adapting to your space is important and also offers an opportunity to provide impact beyond the altar.

"I learned that we always have to adapt ideas for our church," says one volunteer. "We are not the huge cathedral or even a large church. Our ministry is expanding to the environment of the church, not simply altar flowers. The church environment encompasses the outdoors, the narthex or entry transition room, the nave or body of the church, the altar, the music ministry space, and other areas of worship. We are so far focusing on the altar but are gradually going into other areas."

The use of a variety of areas of your sanctuary or foyer for additional design elements can increase opportunities to draw in worshipers and to praise God. We have seen the effective use of candles and props lining the rear of a worship space. These not only complement the altar but can also work with banners hanging in the front and sides of the space and a welcome display in the entrance of the building.

If you have a smaller altar table, you may want to consider designs that overflow onto the area around the altar as needed.

Newer churches are more likely to have more casual, longer tables. These tables offer a great platform for creativity. They also sometimes offer a challenge not to overdo it, using the space merely because the space is available, instead of fitting the design to the image, message, and music.

Try not to get sidetracked by the table design. Work with it. Work around it. One option in working with the altar table is to change the table itself for out-of-the-ordinary occasions. (One church even added wheels to the altar to make moving and storing it easier.)

A recent example of an altar table change at our church occurred during Advent. Pastor Rob requested that the Advent wreath be on the altar table. In the past, the wreath had usually been placed at different places in the front of the church. Mary, in her work with the team, began to search for a distinctive—and evocative—approach. She began to sketch an altar design, trying to figure out how to do a great big Advent wreath on the oblong altar. (Yes, Mary will admit that she even fiddled with this on a church bulletin during services one weekend, determined to find the best approach.)

She finally realized that the altar needed to be completely changed for Advent and that the Tribe could make a table for a special altar. Someone had recently given the church a covered trailer, which was used to store the eleven-foot altar during the Christmas season.

The Tribe constructed a new, round altar using Styrofoam and cinderblocks. With beautiful cloth draped over it, you would never have guessed that the altar was inexpensive and easy to create—requiring no sewing and no power tools. The Tribe placed mixed evergreen branches on the top (freshened with a few new pieces each week) and used large glass cylinders for candles, helping the altar itself become the Advent wreath.

Illustrating another visual approach to worship, the cross on this Advent altar was also new. The Tribe painted the cross with vibrant colors to match a large, painted banner that was placed in our worship area as Advent began. This banner, painted by Cari Bennett Bollinger, is known as a "Mandala painting." Based on symbols from our Christian heritage, the painting centers on a large star that represents God. Everything in the painting points to the sacred center, emphasizing the focus on our Creator. The painting on the cross complemented the painting on the banner, establishing a dramatic visual flow across the front of our worship area.

(In chapter 5, we will offer you more tips on expanding creative design beyond the altar. More information on Cari's art is available in chapter 10. For photos of how these altars look, please see chapter 9 and also take a look at the DVD.)

Approaching altar design with tradition in mind

Throughout ancient and contemporary history, individuals have gathered in community to present their offerings to God, bringing gifts and sacrifices to the altar. Altar-design ministry allows participants to offer another type of gift: their creativity. As one pastor points out, many churches experience the intersection of altar and offering only when the brass offering plates return filled with checks, cash, and change. The altar design provides further convergence of gift and sacrifice.

Your approach to the altar will, of course, depend on the traditions of your church, adapted as appropriate for each tribe. Debate over the purpose of the altar is not limited to this idea of new design. Some purists argue that the altar should be unadorned except for the paraments, a cross, and candles. Others argue that an altar is no longer needed because Christ has atoned for our sins, making a place for a sacrifice unnecessary. For some groups, the table is no longer an altar but a table for the sacrament of Holy Communion.

As you think about your church's altar and how this ministry might work in your setting, consider the words of one altar designer: "I can already hear you—'that's fine in *your* church, but *my* church will *never* go for this!' My advice: Don't be so quick to judge your church; you just might be surprised." She tells of how she thought that people might react negatively when she first helped design different type of altars for an annual church conference. "But I never, never heard even one negative comment! Instead, cameras were produced…and people were taking pictures of the altar, and taking pictures of us with the altar, and asking questions, lots of questions. They got upset when they saw us taking it down because they thought it was all over, only to be appeased when they found out that a new creative altar would take its place."

During the week

Some churches use their sanctuaries for a variety of meetings and activities on weeknights. Depending on events in the worship space you may decide to leave your altar design in place during the week to offer further impact. Not long ago, we heard about a man who goes to a church of a different denomination in our city. He had been attending a weekly men's Bible study at our church and began talking about the altar he gets to see each week. He mentioned how the altar changes from week to week and how, at times, it has answered his questions about the study. On one particular week while his group was debating a question, he looked at the altar "and saw the answer in a cross placed in front of a mirror." Through your ministry, God may touch people you do not even know with altars left in place during the week or moved elsewhere in the building.

In one church, the altar for the upcoming service is usually constructed on the Wednesday evening prior to the weekend service. Many people, including the staff, discern the theme and comment about how it prepares and tugs at their hearts during the days before the worship gathering.

Sometimes during the week a child will move through the sanctuary and arrange things differently. At first this can be annoying, because the design probably needs to be fixed, but the altar designer may realize that the altar image is at work in a young heart, in one who has his or her own vision of God's new creation.

Adapt ideas for use in your church

Whatever the philosophy and heritage of your church, creative design can work. You can find ways to use the altar or communion table, or you can use other areas of the church. A good example of adapting to a particular worship area comes from a woman who attended altar design classes (www.newwinedesign.com) and adapted workroom ideas for a dynamic, new approach in her sanctuary. She placed a long table in the *back* of the church, directed toward the front of the church. On the top of the table she placed loose, blue flat pebbles in the shape of a cross on black fabric. During the service, the pastor asked each person to pick up one of the stones and take it home as a reminder to go out into the world with God's love. "We just took your idea and made it work for us," the woman said. This is a key goal for the altar at your church and for the group you are organizing: Listen for God's guidance, gather ideas, and reshape them to work for your unique congregation.

Ponder these words of encouragement from another church's altar ministry: "I would advise a church to see how meaningful it will make their worship service and if it would fit their church. I would tell them to get started and let God lead them. You will learn more about your own beliefs, you will have fun, and asking will provide the things you need. I have a deeper understanding of the word of God while imagining the altar."

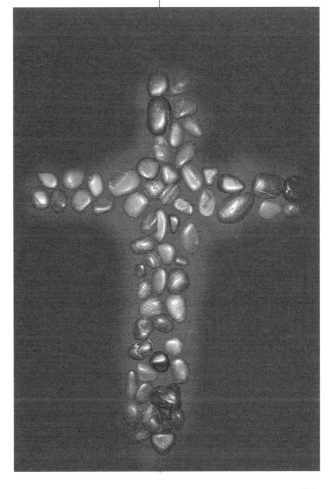

Worksheet: The Altar Table

1. What type of altar table do we have? Can it be changed if needed?

2. What are some of the traditions at our church regarding the altar?

3. How can we integrate altar design into worship?

To pray about: Using the altar for the glory of God in worship.

Notes:

CHAPTER FIVE
The Planning Process

How lovely is your dwelling place, LORD
Almighty! My soul yearns, even faints, for the
courts of the LORD; my heart and my flesh cry
out for the living God. Even the sparrow has
found a home, and the swallow a nest for
herself, where she may have her young—a
place near your altar, LORD Almighty, my King,
and my God. Blessed are those who dwell in
your house; they are ever praising you.

Psalm 84:1-4 (TNIV)

If you walk into many churches during the Advent season, you will notice the color purple or blue used to symbolize truth and eternity. Purple will also be used in many churches during Lent. For Easter, many use white, the color of perfection, beauty, holiness, and joy. And for Pentecost, red symbolizes the Holy Spirit and fire.

Churches that order their worship around the ancient seasons of the Christian year (Advent, Christmas, Epiphany, Lent, Easter, Pentecost) often rely on specific, traditional colors to establish the worship environment. Other churches might think this color key (and the lectionary behind it) is unimportant or too rigid. These altar customs are not biblical guidelines (for example, Christmas was not celebrated until the fourth century), but they have developed through the centuries, and they contribute to the identity of your particular tribe. As you embark on an altar-design ministry, it is important to know what your church's tradition is and whether this can be considered differently.

One of the most spiritually liberating moves in your church will occur when you take powerful and reliable traditions and complement or converge with them with a fresh imagination.

In altar and environment design, it might be an innovation when your congregation begins to follow the church calendar and to use the traditional colors of the Christian year. In other churches, these colors might be blended with colors that suit the taste of the artist. The approach to the colors of your particular Christian (tribal) heritage and the ancient Christian calendar are, like most things, unique to your congregation. Some altar designers believe that God gave us a vivid palette of colors (millions of colors) and that we should use any and all of them. Other churches prefer a more conservative approach. In our congregation, we look for ways to maximize the message of *fewer* colors.

The use of specific colors for specific seasons in the church is an example of a tradition, rather than a scriptural or otherwise divine directive. (You may come across the term *tide* as it relates to combinations of seasons, such as Christmas and the days that follow. Many church traditions developed among European immigrants, who brought their customs over the oceans, including the term *tide*, which means "season.") Some church members may assume that the use of prescribed colors has always been followed, but that is not so. In fact, it is difficult to prove when colors (and other rites) became standardized or regulated. Most worship historians think standardization happened during and following the reign of the fourth-century Emperor Constantine, who required everyone in his empire to become part of the state-run church.

Many churches still plan their services around traditional seasons and colors, but colors can vary according to denomination and the traditions of a church. Some examples are listed below. (For others, see http://www.gbod.org/worship.)

Advent (blue or purple, with one pink candle)

Christmas and Christmastide (white)

Epiphany (green)

Lent (purple)

Maundy Thursday (same as Lent)

Good Friday (black)

Easter and Eastertide (white)

Communion (white)

Pentecost (red)

Special days in the community are also among the special days for churches.

Various churches and denominations have important dates as well, so you may want to fill in the blanks below. Special days that provide opportunities for inventive altar design include:

Sundays in Advent   _____

Christmas Day   _____

New Year's Day   _____

Epiphany   _____

Ash Wednesday   _____

Passion/Palm Sunday   _____

Maundy Thursday   _____

Good Friday   _____

Holy Saturday   _____

Easter Day   _____

Ascension Day   _____

Pentecost   _____

Worldwide Communion Sunday   _____

Thanksgiving Day   _____

Altars offer a canvas upon which to create—a place to take these important and holy days and turn them into something inspirational and visual. You might look for new designs that make use of items other than white candles and brass candlesticks. Perhaps for Pentecost you will cover the altar with forty red candles. Or perhaps you will use beautiful pottery candlesticks for Lent. Or maybe you will call upon an artist in your church to paint something that symbolizes the day.

Remember always to base your designs and your tribal philosophy on biblical principles and metaphors. For example, it is not written in the Bible that Lent must be dominated by dull or somber colors. Springtime and its bright colors usually coincide with Easter, offering the possibility for images from nature that remind us of God's love while helping us reflect on the sacrifice of Christ for our sins.

How to innovate with meaning and purpose

- Consider the key message of each season and the purpose of its celebration.

- Weave those thoughts with possibilities for altar design. Consider the color and texture of the altar cloth you might use or the types of natural materials that might complement the theme.

- Look for areas throughout the worship environment to offer relevant designs.

- Meet with your worship leader to make sure you have the information you need about the service—the sermon, Scriptures, songs, and other worship elements. Consider how the design will work with different parts of the service, such as dance or a new banner for Advent.

- Coordinate your efforts with others as you plan the altar.

- Each piece converges to help people more fully worship God.

How the altar-planning process can work best

Ideally you and your altar team will plan altars for at least six weeks at a time, having a general idea of the focus of the service and the direction of the worship team.

- Do not worry if you are not very organized at this point.

- Ask your worship leader, pastor's assistant, or pastor for upcoming sermon topics and Scripture references for the next six weeks.

- Read each of these Scriptures several times and pray about them.

- Sit quietly and listen for God's guidance in the planning of the altar.

- Get out in the world and look around; explore.

- Be open to the ideas of others.

If your church plans week to week, do not fret

- Acquaint yourself with the church seasons and upcoming events at your church and do some advance work. Then when you get the other information you need, you will already be on the design road.

- If Friday arrives and you do not have the information you need to pull together an idea, pray and wait.

- Pay attention to what you start noticing in the world around you because God may be giving you clues for that week's altar.

- On Saturday, get started with what you know and what you have.

• Stay flexible. Often events at a church or in the world can change plans. Perhaps there will be a big funeral at your church on Saturday morning, for example, or a big world event such as the beginning of a war, or a community tragedy. Such things can immediately change your altar design. (During the writing of this book, Pastor Rob became ill one weekend and at the last minute could not preach. We quickly made small adjustments to the altar to make it more connected to the sermon that would be preached by another pastor.)

Flexibility is required

Everyone knows that the best plans sometimes fall apart and that some churches will not be as organized as others. Circumstances will arise that cause things to be done either at the last minute or with less information than you might have expected. Take a deep breath, and pray. If the moment comes when you must create the altar design and you have no plan, then (1) pray, (2) pay attention to what you see around you, and (3) get started. Consider the objects around you and the items you already have. Think: "What if this becomes the altar?" Often you will get an idea that will not only work but will work well.

Many of the people who go through altar-design training admit that receiving last-minute information from the pastor is a challenge. Not knowing the Scriptures ahead of time is particularly difficult. Sometimes a person becomes ill or has an emergency at the last minute. There are also times when items needed for the design are not available. But these dedicated tribe members move forward with cheerful, servant hearts. As one designer says, you simply beg or borrow, going to someone who knows "just whose yard has that vine." You may be amazed at how often you find materials on the way to church. Somehow the design works out, often better than you could have hoped. Beyond the work on the altar, this flexibility teaches us as Christians to trust God and to forgive others more often in our daily life.

The overall worship environment

The entire worship space provides astonishing alternatives for designing with meaning. You can fully use the unique shape of your whole worship area.

Ways to imagine the whole space:

- Walk slowly into your worship area, and consider options for visually connecting the altar with the back or sides of the space. This could be done with plants or with props, such as containers or rocks.

- Consider the possibility of having a smaller, complementary design as you enter the sanctuary or worship area.

- Look for new ways to enhance the impact, always praying about it and tying it to the meaning of that day's service.

Innovative and worshipful design need not be limited to the main worship area.

- Seize opportunities for designs in the foyer or lobby, in a gathering area or fellowship hall, or in an education building or Sunday school area.

- These designs may be more compact, but they can still have impact.

- They can pull in other volunteers, such as parents and teenagers who work in the youth area or elementary teachers in the children's department.

Outreach opportunities that come through altar preparation

Another joyful blessing sometimes arises in the planning process, when God brings you into contact with those who might need to know about your church or to be reminded of their own relationship with God. This has happened many times in our Tribe while planning and gathering materials for the altar design.

For example, one weekend Pastor Rob wanted "a really big terrarium" to illustrate his message about getting out of our comfort zone and into the world. A visit to a local pet store yielded just what was needed, and it was available for rent. When we returned to pick it up, the owner asked if his son could help with it. "I know you are using this for a church," the father said. "Will you tell my son the same thing you told me about its use?"

The son loaded the terrarium into our vehicle after hearing the story, obviously considering what he heard. "This is for a church, huh? I never dreamed in a million years that we had something that could be used on a church altar." He then began to ask for information about the church. There was a need in his life, and this altar had opened a door.

Another time, a Tribe member was preparing an altar for a service on spiritual gifts. The minister wanted gift boxes, all different sizes and shapes, for the altar. The twenty or so boxes were deliberately gathered at a packing store. As the boxes were stacked, the young adult working at the counter was clearly curious about what the boxes would be used for. "They're going to be on an altar?" she asked, incredulously. The Tribe member gave her a card with information about the church and invited her to come see her boxes on the altar. "I haven't been inside a church for years, and my father was a minister," she said. Another door was beginning to open.

Creative and worshipful altar design often becomes a mixture of these divine moments when God's Spirit works through us to speak to others and more practical moments when details are worked out. Altar designers may feel that they have not been effective witnesses through the years, not telling others about Jesus Christ. But the altar offers opportunities to deliver those messages in a comfortable way.

You control many of the planning details

As you plan altars each week, you should repeatedly pay attention to certain details—such things as materials required, time and volunteers needed to assemble the design elements, cost and availability of props, and other details. Attention to these details will help you adapt to (and shape) the planning habits in your congregation.

Consider using a checklist for this practice so that you do not overlook an important component. At the end of this chapter, we include a checklist that you can copy to keep in a notebook. (Details about assembling such a notebook are found at the end of chapter 7.) Or, you may wish to use our checklist as a guide and design your own.

Worksheet: Altar Design

Date of altar use: _____

Have I prayed about this altar and how it will serve God?

Scripture to be used in the worship service	Music planned for the worship service

What is the theme or focus of this service?

Can the theme be understood as a metaphor, a symbol, or an image? Describe:

Special stories within the sermon (obtained from the preacher or worship coordinator):

Is the sermon part of a series? If so, what element is to be kept each week?

Design concept:

Can this altar-design concept be understood by a variety of ages and people at different
    places in their spiritual lives?   ❏ Yes ❏ No

Do I need help in assembling the altar?   ❏ Yes ❏ No

Will I need help moving or lifting?   ❏ Yes ❏ No

If yes, how many helpers will be needed?

Will I need help taking down the altar?   ❏ Yes ❏ No

When must it be removed?

Supplies needed	Cost	Supplies needed	Cost

Assessment (after the worship event): What would I change? How might it improve?

CHAPTER SIX
The Idea Experience

Trust in the LORD with all your heart and lean
not on your own understanding; in all
your ways submit to him, and he will
make your paths straight.

Proverbs 3:5-6 (TNIV)

One of the most frightening—and yet exhilarating—parts of altar design is coming up with a good, strong idea. The thought of creating an altar basically from scratch causes some to run from the job. But this creation can be inspirational and transforming. Ideas abound. Creation and innovation in worship spaces, for the purpose of serving a holy and loving God, are potent. And remember: There is not a right or wrong way to design an altar, so ideas can cover a wide territory.

Occasionally we take a wrong turn, which we have found out the hard way. As you come up with ideas, it is crucial that you know the theme of the service or message. Our biggest idea blunder—now part of our church lore and appreciated with good humor—involves a horrible miscommunication and the English language, spoken in one of the Southern dialects.

The altar designer that week inquired about the theme of the service and was told the altar needed a yoke in its design. When we arrived at the church that Sunday, the whole altar had been done in yellow and white; the altar designer thought that the pastor had said "yolk."

To complicate matters further, our associate pastor is from Tonga and was still perfecting his English. He also got confused and brought eggs to the children's sermon. So, listen closely as you come up with ideas! (This misunderstanding worked out fine. Pastor Rob tied the mix-up into the sermon and helped us to see the humor in our lives. This is a great example of how loving, supportive, flexible pastors can help a ministry develop by encouraging and guiding.)

How *do* you come up with ideas?

- Once more, prayer is the first step. Ask God for guidance, wisdom, and discernment as you work to serve in your congregation. Take time to listen to how those prayers are answered, and consider ideas that may spring forth from the answers.

- Next, go to the Bible. Read and contemplate the Scriptures that will be used in the upcoming service, particularly the Bible text for that day's sermon. Take notes on the passage; underline words or images that seem especially clear to you. (Be certain that you are using the same version of the Bible as your preacher. In one setting we used a key phrase from a verse on the altar, only to have the pastor read another version—without that key phrase. Each time she referred to the passage, we cringed.)

- If possible, listen to the music that will be sung and played in the service. Drop in to hear the choir or band practice. Borrow the CD or download (but don't steal) the music. Play it on your Walkman or iPod while you pray.

- Read over recent sermons or listen to them on your church's Web site. This will make you more familiar with the preacher's rhetoric and style and will sometimes help you understand where the sermons are going for a period of time.

- If a draft copy or outline of the upcoming sermon is available, study it for insight that will help pull together what the pastor says and how the altar looks.

Since the role of altar designers is to enhance the worship experience, the altar should not stand out in a jarring way. It should not use symbols and props that have nothing to do with that day's sermon and worship theme.
We cannot stress enough that the purpose of innovative altar design is to help make what God is communicating in worship

permanent in the congregation's mind by using a visual tool. Each person will see the altar differently, but the common act of perception can make a wide connection that will draw people together in praise of the Creator.

Wait for the "holy nudge"

Creative, worshipful ideas for altars are in great supply for those who ask God to lead and take time to reflect on the answer. You may even come up with a design by what seems like an accident but may well be a holy nudge. Do not tune out these seemingly wayward thoughts. To do so can keep you from picking up materials you need. We could tell you many stories of favorite "happenstance" altars where we knew a Creator greater than us was at work.

Consider the day when Mary had been unable to come up with an altar design and was driving around town looking for quince, a beautiful bush that is a harbinger of spring in the South. Totally frustrated at not being able to find what she needed, low on gasoline, and running out of time before the service, she turned into her studio parking lot and saw two women sitting in a car. After scurrying inside, Mary picked up what she needed and came out, hoping that they would be gone, thinking about how she did not have time to help them.

There they still sat—an older woman and her very pregnant daughter, car broken down, having waited ages for a taxicab that clearly was not coming. Mary reluctantly asked how she could help. They told her their story and said that they needed to get home—to a dangerous neighborhood. "I'll take you home," Mary said, knowing that she had no cash, that she was running low on gas, and that she really needed to be spending her time on finding some quince or something else for the altar. The neighborhood is considered so unsafe that the woman and daughter wondered whether Mary should be taking them there.

When we pulled up into her driveway, there was the biggest, most beautiful quince blooming. When Mary told the woman what she needed, the woman said, "I'm going to stand and make sure you're okay until you get what you need." The altar was especially awesome that weekend.

Trust God as you design

Time after time, astonishing stories and ideas pop up in the altar-design ministry. By trusting God and listening for divine guidance, many unusual stories will unfold. People from around the country call to tell how something that "just happened" worked out beautifully. Occasionally a fantastic item will be donated at precisely the right moment, such as the holly branches at Christmas, mentioned in the introduction.

Other times, you will miss an opportunity, passing up an item that you will later need. That happened once when we were down to the wire without a plan. Mary, leading the Tribe of Dan, was nearly desperate for something to put on the altar. On their way home from a softball tournament, she and her family were visiting a family farm, where she saw an apple branch loaded with apples. She stopped by the roadside to get it, realized her van was packed full of kids and baseball equipment, and started back on her way, improvising a last-minute design without the branch. When the preacher started the sermon that day, it began with a Scripture reading about Adam and Eve. Mary groaned and looked at her family, knowing she had missed an altar opportunity.

Different perspectives are at work

As you come up with ideas, you will generally have a metaphorical message or symbolic image in mind. Do not be dismayed or surprised at how others interpret the same design. People see and learn from altar designs in ways you would never have imagined, as God speaks to them about a specific area of need in their lives. Sometimes people will get it totally "wrong," according to your perspective, but it will be very much right from theirs.

In addition, as you use new and different materials and props in the worship space, individuals must take a moment or even a few weeks to become familiar with them. This breaking-in period is necessary because often worshipers are in the habit of seeing the same "fancy" items for so long that they no longer actually notice the objects (windows, crosses, pulpit furniture, candles) in the worship space. This tendency for an image or symbolic object to become trite is reminiscent of a friend's expensive coat that she wore continuously because it cost so much. She pulled that "classic" coat out year after year until most of us admitted we were weary of seeing it.

When churches spend large sums of money on different vestments and items for the altar, they feel required to use them, even if the altar no longer seems to enhance worship. What if our friend had not spent much money on her coat? What if it had been a bit trendier? Or reversible? So it goes with altar ideas and the materials you choose to use. Be a good steward of the materials you have, but do not plan an idea around items for the wrong reasons (which might include adoration of the item itself or of the supplier of the item). The transformative altar always points us to God, just as the sermon always affirms a connection between God and us.

As we consider how creative ideas communicate spiritual meaning, ponder the words of a recent student in altar design: "People learn in different ways. Some learn through audio instruction, such as a lecture. Some learn visually; they need to *see* something. I think everyone learns better when a lesson or sermon is presented in many different ways. Probably all churches *read* the Scripture, *speak* the word, and most also experience the lesson with *music*. One thing that is missing in most churches is the specific experience of the visual learning style. What do people *look at* if they learn visually?"

What about ideas that may not be Spirit-led?

Can you get a wrong idea or believe the Holy Spirit is guiding when it is not? Yes, because you are human. But when the Spirit guides, it is usually very direct and sometimes comes booming out of "right field." So, pay attention.

As for wrong ideas, egos will sometimes get in the way, and volunteers can come up with ideas that are not helpful and possibly inappropriate. Sometimes these problems are minor and will slide by and make it into worship, but most of the time they are adjusted by the worship leader or the altar team leader. The pastor and worship director have the authority to change anything on an altar, and altar designers should not have their feelings hurt by their direction. At other times, something you do not like may actually be speaking to someone else—so be aware of the altar ego in you! We can indeed be tempted to go in the wrong direction.

You might also try an idea that does not work, such as an altar we used to illustrate a service about water. We put floating candles into a big, clear bowl that looked great until a candle floated over to the edge of the bowl and the heat met the glass. Normally, loud noises do not come from the altar, but in this case, they did. The pastor walked over and tried to remedy the situation without losing his train of thought. He touched the candle and then touched his microphone, which shorted out the microphone. That was one powerful altar—but not in the way we intended!

On another occasion, a wasp flew out of a large clump of dried grass on the altar and buzzed around the church for a few moments before heading straight for the preacher. The pastor reached up and swatted the insect. Without pausing, he said, "God told us to have dominion over all creatures." He then resumed his sermon, as though nothing had happened.

Suppose an idea will not emerge?

The team is responsible for coming up with altar designs for each service. That does not mean that others will not contribute ideas. Some pastors will regularly have strong opinions on how they want the altar to look for a given sermon or series. At other times, the worship leader will have thoughts. However, the role of the designer is to come up with designs, using those of others when appropriate but not depending on others for ideas each week.

Many of us remember projects on which we had a tough time getting started because the ideas would not come—ranging from term papers in college to arranging the furniture in a new house. In nearly every instance, the best way is to start by taking small step after small step. This often breaks through the idea paralysis that occasionally creeps up on us.

We learn through this process where and when inspiration is most likely to occur, whether early in the morning or late at night, out in nature or at church. In whatever setting works best, let your mind wander and see what emerges. Consider people who inspire you and give you energy; they often will be those persons who you encounter as you come up with ideas. These people provide creative oxygen that helps us live and create to God's glory.

A word of encouragement

Any new endeavor requires training, development, and some trial and error. Be enthusiastic and encouraging during the planning process—both to your team members and to yourself. As time passes, you will find that ideas emerge more naturally. In part, this is because your mind is trained to think about altar design as you go about your daily life, looking for ideas everywhere. In part, it is because you are becoming more familiar with what works and what does not.

As you get started, you might want to be more deliberate in your search for ideas, incorporating the following suggestions into part of your design adventure:

- Take a walk around your yard or neighborhood looking for ideas from nature.

- Stroll through your house with fresh eyes.

- Drive to work a new way to see if roadside materials catch your eye.

- Wander through a fabric store or the fabric department of a department store for inspiration.

- Visit your neighborhood florist to see what types and colors of flowers catch your eye.

- Sit alone in your worship area at church, noticing details such as carpet, windows, and lighting.

- Observe a children's class or a youth meeting and see what ideas come to mind. Perhaps you will find yourself using artwork from a Bible School class or memorabilia from a youth mission trip.

- Visit other churches to see how their altars are designed and how their churches are laid out.

- As your supply area grows, wander through it, studying what is available and considering new ways to use materials on hand. Instead of focusing on what you do not have, be thankful for what you see, and pray about how it can be used.

Any of these tactics can help get the idea factory going in your brain. Do not hesitate to bounce ideas off your altar team members and use their feedback to enhance your designs. Most altar designers like to work together on altars, from planning to execution. This builds community and helps provide awesome altars from the awesome talents coming together for God's work.

Take notes on your ideas, and keep good records of your altar designs. (For more information on keeping an altar journal, see chapter 7.) This practice will keep you from using similar designs all the time and will help you take carefully calculated risks. We like taking risks in altar design and encourage you to use your God-given imagination and creativity. However, risks usually work best when you consider them from a variety of angles and know why you are doing what you are doing, rather than pulling something out of thin air.

Now, time for an idea break. At the end of this chapter, you will find a page for listing ideas you have for altar design. Do not be afraid. They will come to you with God's powerful guidance. God is the master designer.

Worksheet: Altar Design Ideas

1. Favorite visual Scriptures that could be used for an altar design:

2. A list of three to five altar ideas that pop into my mind:

3. Possible altar props to which I have access:

4. Favorite flowers or textiles in my area, and where they are found:

To pray about: God's guidance in developing my creativity and helping me come up with ideas for worshipful altars.

Notes:

CHAPTER SEVEN

A Tool Kit to Get Started

Then the altar will be most holy,
and whatever touches it will be holy.
Exodus 29:37 (TNIV)

Do you remember as a child seeing your father searching for the right tool, frustrated that a certain screwdriver or pair of pliers was out of place? Or recall your teenage years when Dad was sure that you had misplaced his favorite hammer? Most people recall Christmas stories of the toys that could not be assembled because key parts or tools were missing. So it goes with the tools you will need for altar design.

As with most of life's creative efforts, altar design requires the right supplies. The tools need not be fancy or expensive, but they should be reliable and accessible. Your first thought of the supplies you need may very well be flowers or greenery—but be prepared to change your mind. Other, less obvious, supplies will get you going and will stimulate your creativity.

As your ministry begins, you will likely need only the basics. But be prepared! As you become more experienced and decide to take a few more risks with your designs, you will start accumulating many altar materials. The great thing about gathering materials and tools for your altar work is that you will gain new ideas as you pull the items together. You will begin to look at the world around you with new eyes, assessing everything you see with the question: "Would that work on the altar?"

Start with the basics

To be efficient and to keep from being frustrated each time you start putting together an altar, keep at least a small set of tools where you can easily find it. (For years, the trunk of a volunteer's car was the home of our altar tool set.)

Start with a small work/tool box, preferably one that is lightweight with a handle, so you can carry it to and from the altar. Do not forget to write the name of your altar team (such as "Tribe of Dan" at our church) and the name of your church on the toolbox so that you can keep up with it.

In your start-up tool kit, you will need:

- ❏ **Hammer**
- ❏ **Nails, tacks, screws** (assorted sizes)
- ❏ **Screwdrivers** (Flathead and Phillips head)
- ❏ **Florist wire** (assorted sizes)
- ❏ **Several kinds of tape** (Green Oasis florist tape, white and green stem florist tape, clear and duct tape. Like duct tape, masking tape tends to leave a gooey residue on wood, glass, or metal.)
- ❏ **Paint brushes** (1″ and 2″)
- ❏ **Straight pins**
- ❏ **Knife**
- ❏ **Garden shears**
- ❏ **Scissors**
- ❏ **Wire cutters**
- ❏ **Pliers**
- ❏ **Glass cleaner**
- ❏ **Paper towels**
- ❏ **Matches**

As your team grows, and you are more comfortable with altar settings, you may decide to store the following items:

- ❏ **Extra candles and candleholders**
- ❏ **A variety of vases**
- ❏ **Plant saucers and liners**
- ❏ **Small water vials** (to hold individual stems for use in arrangements or overall display)
- ❏ **Flower preservative** (This is optional on your list. We do not find ourselves using it because God always seems to keep the flowers fresh and beautiful.)
- ❏ **Rocks and moss**
- ❏ **Oasis** (Foam blocks that are soaked in water. These will be used to design your flower arrangements. Keep sealed in plastic until ready to use.)
- ❏ **Styrofoam** (This will be useful to wedge under items and to make things stand up straight. This also helps vary heights on items. It is a temporary solution to design dilemmas.)

❏ **Cloth of varied colors to be used as altar draping** (For more information on colors of cloth, please refer to chapter 5.)

❏ **Iron and ironing board** (This is used to press altar cloth. Small travel steam irons are easy to use. We admit that we prefer to use the dryer in the nursery to keep from ironing when possible!)

❏ **Heavy-duty extension cord** (Label the cord with your group's name or it will likely be "borrowed" for use elsewhere.)

❏ **Glue gun or glue skillet with extra glue** (While many people have glue guns, the skillet is a bit less familiar. It is an electric skillet that holds melted glue in which altar props can be dipped. See the DVD for an example.)

❏ **Old towels** (or other rags)

❏ **Buckets** (These will come in handy to provide a variety of heights and to help when removing items, such as used candles, from the altar. The more obvious use is to store cut flowers as you execute your design.)

❏ **Garbage bags**

❏ **Risers—anything that can be used for height variety** (Examples include cinder blocks, bricks, and even books. You might also use small pieces of children's furniture or unpainted craft items like footstools or boxes.)

❏ **Extra fabric to cover containers or naked risers**

❏ **Broom and dustpan** (Again, label with your group name.)

❏ **Vacuum cleaner and extra bags**

❏ **Extra cardboard fabric bolts and cardboard rolls** (These are helpful for storing fabric for multiple uses. This also helps save money and prevents you from having to iron as frequently.)

❏ **Digital camera or Polaroid camera and extra film** (Use this to document your altar designs when they are complete. This will give you a good record for future ideas and will keep you from repeating a design too quickly.)

❏ **Notebook or journal to keep a record of your altar settings** (Store your photos here, and also jot down notes about the Scripture that week or a special story from the sermon. This notebook can become a reference for future design and also can serve as an inspirational guide for altar teams now and yet to come. At the end of this chapter, you will find worksheets to help develop your church's altar team notebook. On the DVD you will find this worksheet, and several worksheets in this book, as Microsoft Word documents. You may prefer to keep your worship design notebook and pictures in a digital format or on a Web site.)

❏ **Calendar of the Christian year and colors of the Christian year** (You might also consider posting a copy of this document—also on the DVD—on your storage room wall. As mentioned earlier, these can be useful in designing relevant altars if your church follows the Christian year and rotates the traditional colors carefully.)

Storage near or next to a sanctuary is a problem for most churches, so you may have to finagle to find a spot for accessories as they accumulate. Some volunteers do designs at home and bring them to the church before services. Or, perhaps you can find a small closet or storage area somewhere at your church where you can install shelves (as some special volunteers did for us). You will know that your altar ministry has arrived when the church management or Altar Guild is willing to add a small annual budget for your supplies. One church crossed this threshold, showing appreciation for a servant attitude, when it set aside storage space and $500 for

altar design supplies. Until then the start-up cost was assumed to be the altar designer's tax-deductible contribution.

In addition to the "extras" that will augment your designs, you will need certain unusual items throughout the year. Many of these items are perishable or seasonal, and you can pick them up as they are needed. Others will become part of your altar inventory.

Items that will make up the heart of your designs:
Fresh flowers and greenery. The possibilities here are limitless, and items can be picked up at local florist shops, grocery stores,

sidewalk vendors, and wholesale warehouses. (For more information, please see chapter 10.) We believe that all items on the altar should be real, not artificial. The use of fresh flowers and greenery is a sacrifice we make to honor God as we worship.

Area florists and stores are often generous in donating—or selling at clearance prices—flowers that may be a bit past their prime. Many of these are still beautiful and work well on the altar, even though they require a bit more design effort. As we were writing this book, we received leftover roses that had not sold at Valentine's Day. An older church member happened to be waiting for a meeting to start when the altar was being assembled, and he volunteered to help. He was given the tedious job of peeling brown petals off the outside of the blooms. The next day he contacted us to say how meaningful that small job had been. As he peeled away ugly and dying petals, the beautiful core of the blossom was revealed, reminding him of how we so often judge people by the outside when the inside is beautiful and of how God loves us all the way to our inner being.

Wild flowers and weeds...yes, especially weeds. Some of the most beautiful altar designs incorporate unconventional items, such as black-eyed Susans that grow by the side of the road in the South. Johnson grass, a weedy looking grass that is despised by farmers and lawn jockeys, has a lot of height and character. The plants we find by the side of the road (which we affectionately call "roadsidia") often adorn the altar with great character and creativity.

One sermon topic referred to God giving refuge to those in need. On a short road trip with a friend, the idea for the altar design appeared—in the form of palmetto leaves growing by the side of the road. We carefully gathered the leaves, and later fashioned them into a shelter so inviting that a church staff member approached the altar and sat underneath the branches before the service began. (We remind you to use caution when stopping by the side of the road for materials.)

Do not be afraid to stop and knock on doors if you see something that might be useful—being aware of your surroundings, of course. Always ask permission before taking materials from what could be private property. Politely ask if you can buy some of the flowers or greenery for the church altar. Often you will find that people are delighted to have something from their yard used on an altar and are happy to give you the items. If someone turns you down, say thanks and move on to a new plan.

An example of finding such flowers in our community is the time we discovered a beautiful wild-looking plot of jonquils that burst forth each spring. The lot is adjacent to a building that looks vacant. Mary went to the door and knocked, and knocked, and knocked.

Finally, the door slowly creaked open to reveal a tiny, elderly man who said that his wife, who had died, planted the flowers and that many people came to pick them without asking. "I appreciate you knocking on the door and asking me about them," he said. "My wife would be pleased that they're going to be on the altar."

The man donated flowers for several years, and then one year there was no answer at the door. Mary left a thank-you note on his door and later saw one of his children cleaning up around his place. The daughter said he had gone to a nursing home and that he loved the fact that "those flowers every spring were used on a church altar." This was a special relationship that involved someone who never stepped foot in our church but added greatly to worship through his gift of spring flowers.

Of course, gathering materials does not always bring such a warm feeling. Take, for instance, the student in an altar-design class who gives us a reminder to be careful while gathering materials in the wild. The fall day was beautiful, and the students were in the woods, having been warned to watch for snakes and cautioned against the beautiful leaves that grow straight up—poison ivy. As the students wrapped up their excursion and prepared to assemble the altar, one student returned with arms outstretched, full of large orange and yellow leaves—poison ivy. No warm feeling here—only a lot of powerfully annoying itching in the days ahead. (This incident reminds us of sin, by the way. We are warned against it; it has been described to us; but we just can't resist.)

Fresh fruits and vegetables. These relatively inexpensive items can add much to an altar and integrate with many different messages. Our Tribe of Dan actually spends more on fruits and vegetables than on fresh flowers. Again: Avoid artificial items.

A collection of crosses. Beyond the traditional brass cross, be on the lookout for unique crosses that fit with a theme or message. Know that you will probably not find many ready-made crosses that are the right proportion for your altar. You might find that you enjoy making your own crosses. One of our favorites is a cross that is constructed of brightly colored tin fish. This cross works well with a variety of sermon topics and always generates comments from the congregation. It is made of recycled oil drums that were sent to Haiti to be made into items that are resold. The metal was painted into colorful fish and put on a panel. We purchased one at a wholesale nursery show, had it cut in two, and welded it back together as a cross. This cross is so brightly colored that we considered it a risk for our design—but it has turned out to be a favorite and has been used for national conferences in a variety of ways. Sometimes you fret over an idea, and it turns out better than you could hope.

Personal items. Altar designers regularly find items in their cabinets and closets that make terrific altar props. As Tribe member Annie mentioned earlier, her collection of saris and shawls is often used. Another member tells of using her collection of pots, blankets, and other items from Mexico for an altar that coincided with a youth mission trip to Mexico.

Odds and ends. Altar items will begin to pop up everywhere when you start noticing all the possibilities. Seeds will be planted and will sprout when you see something that will add to a design on the altar. Sometimes you will not know how an item will be used, but you will know that you need to add it to your collection. Then later it will be a key symbol for an upcoming service. Your instincts will serve you well here.

Be willing to use new items on your altar if they are in keeping with the message of the service or if they speak to you in a strong way. Recall the biblical words at the beginning of this chapter; objects take on holy and new meaning when they are placed upon the altar.

Snow skis formed one of the most unusual crosses we ever made. The cross was used during youth worship services on a ski trip. Subsequently used on the church's main altar, the cross now hangs in the youth department throughout the year and goes with the youth each year on their trip.

A part-time pastor and his daughter designed another favorite cross. It is a dramatic cross covered in oversized nails—except the nails are actually dowel rods, carefully painted so that an observer cannot tell the difference.

Still another cross is painted with the silhouette of Bethlehem. White Christmas lights provide the stars in the night sky. We drilled holes in the cross, and randomly inserted the lights for a dramatic effect. (This cross is shown on the DVD.)

As you accumulate supplies and try new altar designs, having a record of what has been done will be helpful. Keep a notebook of altar designs to help shape future efforts and to teach new people how to be part of the ministry. A simple three-ring binder with unlined paper works well. (A sample format for such a notebook is included at the end of this chapter.)

Tucked behind the worship area and shared with musical and electronic equipment, the storage closet at our home church provides both practical space to put materials and inspiration for future altars. This storage area is not the neatest part of the church, but it may be one of the most used areas. As altar designers walk into this cluttered, creative area, they begin to imagine an upcoming altar design and its possibilities, put together with this motley array of tools and supplies.

We hope that you will find, as we have, that tools will come together to help your altars function as tools themselves—worship tools.

Worksheet: Putting Together a Useful Notebook

1. **Make at least one page for each week**. On these pages you will glue photos of your work and sketches of your ideas and notes about the altar.

2. **Include the Scripture reading and the topic and theme of the sermon for that day**.

3. **Write what you learned from this altar design and what you would do differently if you were to use the design again**.

4. **List how much you spent on the items.** (Be honest and note when you think you spent too much for the results.) This will help you build an accurate budget as time goes on.

5. **Other sections of the book may include:**
   - **A list of group members, e-mail addresses, phone numbers, and addresses.** This will be particularly useful when a member needs to trade weekends with another member.
   - **A copy of the Christian calendar and the accompanying color chart** (if your church follows this calendar or colors).

6. **Keep a copy of each Tribe member's signed commitment sheet to this team and to the process.** (For a copy of this sheet, see the end of chapter 3.)

To pray about: How this ministry can become part of the meaningful traditions of your church.

Notes:

Altar Designs

Team Contacts

Commitment Forms

Suppliers

Calendar and Colors

CHAPTER EIGHT

Let the Creation Begin

Let the heavens rejoice, let the earth be glad;
let them say among the nations, "The LORD
reigns!"

1 Chronicles 16:31 (TNIV)

Pray. We will keep reminding you that this is the first step as you begin to create an altar. This should never vary. Prayer is the foundation upon which an awesome altar will be built. From here, you begin the joyful process of creating.

Let's walk together through the conception and design of an altar, taking a look at some of the principles you will need, and having fun with the inspiration that comes forth.

When you begin to assemble your altar design, focus on the Scripture passage that will be used in the service. If you have not done so, stop and reflect. These Bible verses provide information you need about the theme of the message.

Consider as an example the Acts 3 story about a crippled beggar who asks two disciples for money. The disciples have no money, but they heal the man and tell him to stand and walk in the name of Christ. We could not begin to design the most appropriate altar without Scripture as a reference point. (The resulting altar, entitled Bent Out of Shape, is shown on the accompanying DVD and is explained in our how-to sampler in chapter 9.)

Where to find visual hints

As you consider the Scripture references each week, look for a visual hint. This will likely be one of the most important elements in the story, something that jumps out at you. In the story from Acts 3, for instance, a useful image is that of "standing straight." Another is of the disciples headed to prayer.

From here, find out what music will be a part of the service. Listen to it if possible, or read the words. (If your church does not put the words to songs on a screen, or does not sing from a hymnal, this element is not as important. It is often difficult for people in the congregation to understand all of the words in a song, if they are not seeing them.)

Your next level of inspiration might be a story that will be used in the sermon. This is usually obtained directly from the preacher or through the worship director.

Through this process, ideas will likely converge. (If you are struggling, remember the steps for ideas that we walked through in chapter 6.)

How a cross will be used

The most important item on many altars is the cross. Exceptions to this generalization occur when a large cross adorns the front of the sanctuary, when church traditions steer away from use of a cross, or when some Christian symbols are intentionally subdued in a "seeker" worship service. Sometimes the design of the worship area may dictate not using a cross on the altar because it might block the view of the choir. If you are going to use a cross on your altar table, consider how it can best be displayed and incorporated into the overall theme of the service.

You must decide if you will use a cross already on hand—including the possibility of turning it around for a different look. You can also consider having someone make a cross for an altar. We have used many unusual and handcrafted crosses, often designed by people in our congregation. This offers yet another way for people to use their creativity as a gift to their church.

It may take you a while to get comfortable with the idea of different sorts of crosses, but do not become paralyzed by this reluctance. Instead, find a cross with which you are comfortable and move ahead.

Other parts of the service and how they affect the altar

As you choose items to place on the altar, consider how other parts of the service, such as a liturgical dance, may affect the design. What effect will these have on the attitude or feeling you are trying to convey?

Many altars incorporate cloth of some type. The variety is as great as the ideas you will come up with over the years. As you choose fabric, consider the season of the year. Keep in mind that lightweight fabric is usually better for spring and summer, and heavier fabric is usually better for fall and winter. Remember also to look at the many details of the service. For example, in the story found in Acts 3, the disciples say they have no silver or gold. Therefore, it is better not to use silver or gold cloth or brass candlesticks on the altar, thereby creating visual confusion. Imagine the setting of the story and how the people in the verses might have looked. In this case, consider that the two disciples and the beggar were roughly dressed, which might lead to an altar design that has a rougher texture.

The use of candles

Selecting a candle or candles and accompanying candlesticks is another layer of your design. Many altars will need a candle, but this depends upon your denomination and church tradition. The altar requires a candle for the acolyte to light in many denominations. Avoid the habit of always using white candles; this change can help your altar become more interesting and inviting.

Research into manuals for the Altar Guild does not turn up a particular formula for use of candles on altars. Some interpreters say we have two candles, one for the Old Testament and one for the New. Others say it represents Christ as a human and Christ as God. The use of candles is symbolic and probably evolved from traders selling what they had many centuries ago. Pray about this, and consider the heritage of your church. Be open to new ways to help move worshipers without relying on something that may have lost its meaning for your church. (For more information on types of candles, see chapter 10.)

As you assemble your design, consider certain principles:

- Is the altar message simple? Can all ages and education levels get something out of it?

- Props of all kinds can tell a story quickly. Many of these are unconventional, ranging from rocks to wood to cardboard.

- Different age groups respond to different colors. For example, older congregants tend to need brighter, more visible colors. Younger congregants are much more flexible in color selection.

- White fabric will overwhelm many other elements, so use it sparingly. It captures the eye's attention immediately and can prevent you from noticing other details. (This is why emergency vehicles, such as ambulances, are often white.)

- If your church broadcasts services, or projects live camera imagery during services, how will the altar look on camera? Do you have, for example, a dark cloth against a dark backdrop that obscures major parts of the design?

- Is the proportion of elements in balance? You do not want to use a huge cross and one tiny candle, for example.

- Can the design be seen from the back of the church? Again, candles should be high enough that back-row worshipers can see them. Clusters of items, such as votives, can provide added impact.

- Extra lighting on the altar is important but should work with other elements of the service. Does the lighting wash out a screen for image projection? Does it cast shadows on the preacher's face? (On the DVD, you can see an example of before-and-after lighting.)

- Can this design be done within the group's budget, and can items have more than one use? This adds good stewardship to good design.

Back to prayer

After you have considered these principles and come up with an idea, pray again before you begin to execute the idea. Listen closely for God's voice in the process before you go further.

Then, begin putting together the altar. Make sure you have your tools and materials handy. This is where your unique creative gifts can really shine and be enjoyable in the process.

One of the great blessings of altar design is that it allows creative souls to shine through, speaking God's message through gifts that may previously have been untapped. We think of an altar volunteer who struggled with low self-esteem and with fitting into the body of Christ. She grew in confidence as she was allowed to try altar designs. "Creativity can only flourish where the people themselves are nourished and given the freedom to make mistakes and grow," she says.

Remember: The altar is an offering that you give in order to help draw people toward God. Don't worry about perfection—just do the best that you can!

Worksheet: Creating

1. Have I prayed about each altar I am working with? Do I pray for God's hand in my work?

2. Am I reflecting upon Scripture passages and prayerfully considering their meaning and possibilities for altar design?

3. Am I open to suggestions and ideas from others?

To pray about: Insight from the Bible and guidance from the Holy Spirit.

Notes:

CHAPTER NINE

Altar Examples You Can Adapt for Your Church

Two are better than one, because they have a
    good return for their labor:
If they fall down, they can help each other
    up.
But pity those who fall and have no one to
    help them up!
                       Ecclesiastes 4:9-10 (TNIV)

Sharing altar ideas with you is a great joy. Some of the designs may work nearly exactly as they are shown here. Or, you may change them quite a lot. All can be adapted for different worship shapes and spaces, different altar tables, different traditions, and different genres (e.g., traditional, Celtic, Taizé, seeker, Latino, jazz, and any other forms) of worship. We attempt to offer a broad variety to help you with ideas and different approaches, and we have explained many of them in more detail on the DVD. You can see each of these altars in an enlarged, color format on the DVD in the Altar Examples section. Each of these has been used in a service, so we know they all *can* work. However, they may not all work for you. Do not be afraid to adjust them or to pick and choose from them.

These samples can be used with a variety of Scriptures and service themes. We suggest possible Scriptures but encourage you not to be limited by them. These altar designs can work with many different verses and Bible stories. Also, sometimes altars will vary based on the music that will be used during a service. When all of these elements weave together, altars often have the greatest impact. We are providing you with samples that have been done on both large and small altar tables to help you see the possibilities. We also offer ideas of other places you might try these in your church.

Use your imagination as you envision these altars. Let us know how they work for you. Tell us your ideas. May we help each other along the way as we seek to tell others about Jesus Christ and the God we worship.

Oversized Advent Altar Wreath

Season of use: Advent

Suggested Scripture reference: Luke 2:1-20 (the birth of Christ)

Theme or special focus of the service: Weeks leading up to Christmas, Advent sermon series, or special services

Design concept: Do the unexpected. We wanted to do something totally different from what we had done in the past. We have had the Advent wreath on the altar before, so we thought, "Why not make the entire altar table the Advent wreath?"

Number of team members needed to assemble altar: Four to ten

Supplies needed:

- Two sheets (4′ x 8′) of wall insulation
- Purple fabric three times the circumference of the table (We selected fleece because we wanted to have a soft fabric left over to make throws to sell in the youth auction.)
- Six yards of pink fabric for top of table (You will be a little short of fabric, but there will be enough left over after cutting the circle to fill in the tiny space left to one side of the table. Not to worry—greenery will cover that area anyway.)
- Five glass cylinders
- Five glass oil holders
- Smokeless lamp oil
- Five green six-inch wooden florist picks
- Readymade garland (We used a 75′ garland, because we wanted it extremely full, but 50′ would work fine. Try to buy it wholesale from a floral-supply house.)
- Styrofoam (Try to buy it from a local plastic-supply house.)

Style of worship area and altar size: This particular altar requires a bit more space than some. It could be placed to the side of a sanctuary, given less space near the front. A smaller version could also be made.

Special notes: Fabric is the biggest expense. This altar is not as tough to design as it looks. We got a late start on this and wondered where we would get an eight-foot round table and that much purple fabric. We also did not know if we had time to pour four huge pink and purple candles. (For information on recycling candles, see the DVD.)

Candle Screen

Season of use: Any (depending upon the season, you may want to use different fabric colors)

Suggested Scripture reference: "Therefore, I urge you, brothers and sisters, in view of God's mercy, to offer your bodies as a living sacrifice, holy and pleasing to God—this is true worship. Do not conform to the pattern of this world, but be transformed by the renewing of your mind. Then you will be able to test and approve what God's will is—his good, pleasing and perfect will" (Romans 12:1-2, TNIV).

Theme or special focus of the service: Program or sermon on seeking God's will. (This was used for a class for people trying to discern God's call to the ministry and also for weekend worship services.)

Design concept: Not making the cross highly visible to those in attendance. We wanted them to search for it, symbolic of searching for God's will.

Number of team members needed to assemble altar: Two to three

Supplies needed:
- Metal framework
- Votive candles
- Plants (we used six prayer plants)
- Native tallow berries
- Pebbles
- Recyclable fabric

Style of worship area and altar size: Any. This is shown on an eleven-foot altar but could be scaled down.

Other ideas: Use a stronger-color cross for other seasons, red candles for Pentecost.

Special notes: Lighting this many candles takes a long time, and the candles are hot. Let them cool down before moving them off the altar and do not put fabric on or over them, because it is a fire hazard. (Always be careful when you place items near candles.)

Triumphant Entry

Season of use: Palm Sunday

Suggested Scripture reference: Matthew 21:1-10 "Hosanna to the son of David! Blessed is he who comes in the name of the Lord!" (Matthew 21:9, NRSV)

Theme or special focus of the service: The weekend before Easter

Design concept: Simplicity. Use of plain green cloth with palm fronds painted on it. Coordinate with children marching in waving palm fronds.

Number of team members needed to assemble altar: One or two

Supplies needed:
- Green fabric—size depends on the size of your altar
- Black and purple spray paint (Put leaf on fabric and spray over it.)
- Purple kale
- Cross
- Candles

Style of worship area and altar size: Any, but works quite well in an auditorium or theater-style setting. This altar should be in the front of the worship area. The example shown here is designed for a five-and-one-half-foot altar.

Other ideas: Palm plants can be bought inexpensively and used on either side of the altar. However, because they are difficult to keep alive, you will probably want to plan on using the plants only on this occasion.

The Butch Box

Season of use: Any

Suggested Scripture reference: Any verses on tithing or prayer

Theme or special focus of the service: A service in which the congregation is called upon to participate in one of many ways: Commitment Day with pledge cards, prayer requests, giving up worries, suggestions for moving ministries forward.

Design concept: Worshipers come forward and make a commitment or offer up a prayer or concern.

Number of team members needed to assemble altar: One or two

Supplies needed:

- Container in which participants can place items (The photograph shows a box handcrafted by a church member. This box was originally intended to house a projector. Another special container could also be used.)
- Fabric
- Greenery
- Candle

Style of worship area and altar size: Any. This works very well with a large or small altar. The example shown here is designed on a five-and-one-half-foot altar.

Other ideas: Divide altar into ten sections using fabric or tape to make stripes, perhaps coloring-in 10 percent of the fabric. This helps illustrate the vast difference between the 10 percent we give to God and the 90 percent we keep.

Special note: We find that services with an interactive component that includes the altar are particularly powerful.

Thirst No More

Season of use: When weather is hot, so people are reminded of a cool, refreshing place

Suggested Scripture reference: John 4:10-14
"Everyone who drinks of this water will be thirsty again, but those who drink of the water that I will give them will never be thirsty. The water that I will give will become in them a spring of water gushing up to eternal life" (John 4:13-14, NRSV).

Theme or special focus of the service: Renewal, a seasonal summer series, or a sermon on one of many references to water in the Old and New Testaments

Design concept: Use of running water during service; oasis amidst the desert

Number of team members needed to assemble altar: Three

Supplies needed:

- Shells

- Water pump

- Wooden cross

- Dried grasses

- Sand

- Candles

- Fabric

- Erosion cloth (used in highway construction)

Style of worship area and altar size: If you do not have a good place at the front of the church to put a fountain, this design could be set to the side or put in the foyer or lobby. This also could be used for Vacation Bible School worship or commencement. It makes a great participatory setting for children, who can pick up sand or shells or bring a shell to the altar. This example is designed on an eleven-foot altar.

Other ideas: The cost of a fountain can vary; it is possible that someone in your congregation can make one (as we did here). The pump supplies can be found at one of the big-box hardware or home improvement stores. Or, perhaps you will decide to invest more money in a fountain if you will be using it frequently. This is the kind of item that will likely be worth your investment.

On the DVD you will notice that there are several sample altars incorporating the fountain. We have used it for weddings, funerals, and a multitude of sermons. Children love it!

Break Bread Together

Season of use: Any

Suggested Scripture reference: Mark 14:21-23
"While they were eating, he took a loaf of bread, and after blessing it he broke it, gave it to them, and said, 'Take; this is my body'" (Mark 14:22, NRSV).

Theme or special focus of the service: Communion

Design concept: An abundance of grapes and bread representing elements of communion, which symbolize the body (broken for you) and blood (shed for you) of Jesus Christ

Number of team members needed to assemble altar: One or two

Supplies needed:

- Real grapes (*never* fake, please!)

- Loaves of bread (Buy day-old loaves of bread for display on the altar, or, even better, ask a local store to donate the old bread.)

- Wheat

- Fabric

- Cross

Style of worship area and altar size: Any. The example shown here is designed on a five-and-one-half-foot altar.

Other ideas: We suggest that your church consider having more than one set of Communion serving pieces (chalice and patten/plate). This offers a variety of looks that can be coordinated with each Communion service.

If you use stackable holders for individual Communion cups, consider draping them with fabric that has an ancient look and removing the fabric as part of the introduction of Communion.

Some churches practice Communion by intinction, with individuals going to the front of the church to dip the bread into the cup. This offers people an opportunity to draw close to the altar and to participate more fully in worship, adding to the impact of a Communion service.

World Communion Day

Season of use: World Communion Day

Suggested Scripture reference: 1 Chronicles 16:24, Mathew 28:19

"Declare his glory among the nations, his marvelous works among all the peoples" (1 Chronicles 16:24, NRSV).

"Go therefore and make disciples of all nations, baptizing them in the name of the Father and of the Son and of the Holy Spirit" (Mathew 28:19, NRSV).

Theme or special focus of the service: Worldwide community of Christ, as people everywhere share Communion

Design concept: Flags of the nations, attached to a cross made of Styrofoam, with bread speared on plastic plant stakes

Number of team members needed to assemble altar: One or two

Supplies needed:
- Breads
- Styrofoam cross
- Flags
- Reusable plant (We've used the plant pictured for six years. Be sure to keep your older plants fertilized and watered, so they look healthy.)
- Fabric

Style of worship area and altar size: Any. This will hold up well in a small space. It also could be compelling in the entry area of your church. This one is on an eleven-foot altar table.

Other ideas: Foreign flags are usually available in education-supply stores. Several online stores carry international flags (e.g., usflags.com). One church near two universities in Nashville has members from twenty-five countries. On Worldwide Communion Sunday they drape these twenty-five flags from the balconies, illustrating how the altar is part of the entire worship environment and how the people of God are disciples from many nations.

Rock of Ages

Season of use: Any

Suggested Scripture reference: Mark 14:32-42 "They went to a place called Gethsemane; and he said to his disciples, 'Sit here while I pray.' He took with him Peter and James and John, and began to be distressed and agitated. And he said to them, 'I am deeply grieved, even to death; remain here, and keep awake.' And going a little farther, he threw himself on the ground and prayed that, if it were possible, the hour might pass from him" (Mark 14:32-35, NRSV).

Theme or special focus of the service: This altar can be used for very different types of messages. It can illustrate letting Christ rock our world and change our lives, or it can remind worshipers of the steadiness of Jesus.

Design concept: The rocks are intended to draw in the worshiper with the sense of a place of holiness, an ancient and peaceful presence.

Number of team members needed to assemble altar: One or two

Supplies needed:

- Plywood

- Rocks (the rocks, purchased at a wholesale market, are glued one on top of the other)

- Recyclable oil lamps, made of rock

- Flowers

- Fabric

Style of worship area and altar size: Any. You will notice that this example shows how to build a beautiful altar without an altar table.

Other ideas: Rocks are mentioned throughout the Bible and are great for regular use on the altar.

We have accumulated a rock pile behind the church. These rocks come and go, showing up in Sunday school classrooms and throughout the church. This cross is quite heavy and not easy to move.

Music often ties in with the theme of the altar, and we use this one as an example. "Jesus is the Rock" is the song that we focused on during this particular service.

You could put rocks in containers near the doors for worshipers to take home as a reminder of the service. A pile of rocks could be incorporated into existing areas, such as planters or at the base of tables at the entrance of the church.

Bent Out of Shape

Season of use: Any, but particularly effective during Lent

Suggested Scripture reference: Luke 13:10-17—The story of the woman, bent by illness and healed by Jesus, and the indignant Pharisees who were bent out of shape by the healing.

"She was bent over and could not straighten up at all. When Jesus saw her, he called her forward and said to her, 'You are set free from your infirmity.' Then he put his hand on her, and immediately she straightened up and praised God" (Luke 13:11-13, TNIV).

Theme or special focus of the service: A series on miracles, a service about prayer, a service of introspection about what bends us out of shape in our own lives

Design concept: The items on the altar all have a crooked or bent component.

Number of team members needed to assemble altar: One or two

Supplies needed:
- Bean pods
- Dried plant material with curves
- Curved candles
- Fabric

Note: This cross is made from different types of dried beans glued onto a wooden cross in a wavy pattern. Pieces of altar cloth are also glued into the pattern to provide depth.

Style of worship area and altar size: Any. This example is designed on an eleven-foot altar.

Pentecost

Season of use: Pentecost, seven weeks after Easter

Suggested Scripture references: John 15:26, Acts 2:1-4

"When the Advocate comes, whom I will send to you from the Father, the Spirit of truth who comes from the Father, he will testify on my behalf" (John 15:26, TNIV).

"When the day of Pentecost had come, they were all together in one place. And suddenly from heaven there came a sound like the rush of a violent wind, and it filled the entire house where they were sitting. Divided tongues, as of fire, appeared among them, and a tongue rested on each of them. All of them were filled with the Holy Spirit and began to speak in other languages, as the Spirit gave them ability." (Acts 2:1-4, TNIV).

Theme or special focus of the service: The wonder of Pentecost

Design concept: Recreating the flames of Pentecost

Number of team members needed to assemble altar: One or two

Supplies needed:
- Cast iron plants
- Paint
- Fabric
- Candles

Style of worship area and altar size: Any. This example is designed on an eleven-foot altar.

Other ideas: After you use this, you could recycle it by displaying it in a Sunday school facility or education building.

Some churches only celebrate Pentecost Sunday, while others may keep the red paraments up a while longer. If you are unsure about this, ask your pastor or refer to a Web site, such as www.gbod.org.

Wedding

Season of use: Any

Suggested Scripture reference: I Corinthians 13 (The "love chapter")

Theme or special focus of the service: Focuses on love during a wedding ceremony, but also can be used for a marriage enrichment or renewal emphasis

Design concept: Reversible cross of gold and silver is the dominant object.

Number of team members needed to assemble altar: One to three

Supplies needed:
- Cross
- Flowers
- Candles
- Fabric

Note: The items for the altar depend on the bride and groom, their budget, and color scheme.

Style of worship area and altar size: Any. This example is designed on an eleven-foot altar.

Other ideas: During one wedding, bridesmaids placed lit candles on the altar as they came to the front of the service.

Special note: If your altar-design team is asked to help with a wedding, be aware that by doing it "just this one time," you are getting your group into uncharted and often troubled waters. You may want to establish a special-events policy for your Tribe. If you do help with weddings, details and expenses should be worked out well in advance. In our experience, the bride's family usually pays for flowers and, thus, a special altar for a wedding. Your altar-design policy should be included in any packet concerning weddings at your church.

Check with the wedding party to see if they will allow items to be reused by the altar design team after the wedding. Wedding flowers can rarely be used exactly as they are, so you will probably need to take apart the arrangements for use on that week's altar.

Fruit of the Spirit

Christian behavior

Season of use: Summer or harvest

Suggested Scripture Reference: Galatians 5:22-23

"By contrast, the fruit of the Spirit is love, joy, peace, patience, kindness, generosity, faithfulness, gentleness, and self-control. There is no law against such things" (Galatians 5:22-23, NRSV).

Theme or special focus of the service: Anticipation of God's blessings, gratitude,

Design concept: Colorful, fresh fruit helps you realize that a tree has gone through an entire cycle. A tree must go through a dormant period, budding, blooming, and producing. Each bloom becomes the fruit.

Number of team members needed to assemble altar: One or two

Supplies needed:
- Fabric
- Fresh fruit
- Glass cylinders
- Cross (The cross shown is made of wooden rosettes purchased from a hardware store; a woodworker with a router bit can produce the same thing.)
- Candles

Style of worship area and altar size: Any. Works very well in any size worship area and can be effective off to the side. The example shown here is designed on a five-and-one-half-foot altar.

Other ideas: This altar is an excellent example of how you can use varying sizes of altar tables with no loss of impact. While the example shown was created on a long table, in the DVD you will see that a small table is just as effective.

Funeral Service

Season of use: Any. Can be used on All Saints' Sunday, which is the first Sunday after Halloween. Halloween in the sacred calendar means, "all hallows' eve," in reference to the ordinary saints of a congregation, who have gone to be with the Lord (Hebrews 11).

Suggested Scripture reference: Psalm 23, Luke 23:42-43
"The LORD is my shepherd, I shall not want.
He makes me lie down in green pastures;
  he leads me beside still waters;
    he restores my soul.
He leads me in right paths
  for his name's sake.
Even though I walk through the darkest valley,
  I fear no evil;
  for you are with me;
  your rod and your staff—
  they comfort me"
(Psalm 23:1-4, NRSV).

"Then he said, 'Jesus, remember me when you come into your kingdom.' He replied, 'Truly I tell you, today you will be with me in Paradise'" (Luke 23:42-43, NRSV).

Theme or focus of the service: Funeral or memorial service

Design concept: This is a soothing altar that remembers a special person. It can include photographs and memorabilia.

Number of team members needed to assemble altar: One or two

Supplies needed:
• Fabric
• Candles

- Plants (You might want to use birds of paradise or weeping willow branches.)
- Cross

Note: The supplies will depend upon the verses you choose as well as upon the person whose life you are remembering.

Style of worship area and altar size: Any. This example is designed on an eleven-foot altar.

Other ideas: One church puts up pictures in church for one year (all in matching frames) of all who died that year. Many times, especially in larger churches, pictures are helpful to other churchgoers who may not have known that person by name but knew him or her by sight.

If you design an altar for a funeral or memorial service, other plants and flowers need to be placed to the side or in the foyer or taken to the cemetery. Otherwise, the simplicity of the altar is overwhelmed.

Tapestry Cross

Season of use: Fall or winter

Suggested Scripture reference: Leviticus 16:11-13, Matthew 2:11

"[And he shall] put the incense on the fire before the LORD, that the cloud of the incense may cover the mercy seat that is upon the covenant, or he will die" (Leviticus 16:11-13, NRSV).

"Then, opening their treasure chests, they offered him gifts of gold, frankincense, and myrrh" (Matthew 2:11, NRSV).

Theme or special focus of the service: Teaches congregation about traditional elements long forgotten from the ancient text

Design concept: A more formal occasion, or in any traditional worship setting

Number of team members needed to assemble altar: One or two

Supplies needed:
- Candles
- Candleholders
- Plants
- Fabric
- Incense holder (This is usually available at local import stores. It is difficult to find the incense and charcoal you need from mall stores. You can also find it at Cokesbury stores or www.Cokesbury.com.)

• Tapestry (We used a piece of ready-made tapestry and stretched it over batting and two-inch Styrofoam insulation. This type of insulation is what you will find at a specialty plastics store.)

Style of worship area and altar size: Any. Very effective in traditional and more formal spaces but also can add a new dimension to a contemporary approach to worship in theater-style surroundings. This example is designed on an eleven-foot altar.

Other ideas: This approach is a good example of an altar that might be explained in the bulletin. It might also be part of a church discussion on traditions and prejudices.

You could involve more people in the service by having acolytes carry in incense.

This altar setting could also be used for a winter wedding. (Can you see burgundy and green velvet bridesmaids' dresses with this?)

Cracked Pots

Season of use: Any

Suggested Scripture reference: Isaiah 61:1*b*
"He has sent me … to bind up the broken-hearted" (Isaiah 61:1*b*, NRSV).

Theme or special focus of the service: This image can be used for a multitude of themes, including how God uses us in our brokenness, how we are healed, how we are made one in Christ, and more. Have fun coming up with a variety of uses for this design.

Design concept: Broken pieces of terracotta reassembled into the shape of a cross

Number of team members needed to assemble altar: One or two

Supplies needed:

• Plain wooden cross (Spray paint this cross a dark color.)

• Broken flowerpots (Glue the pieces onto the cross.)

• Marine epoxy glue (This adhesive is available at most hardware stores and is needed to secure the pottery onto the wood. Hot glue, dispensed from a gun or dipped from a skillet, will not work. When the room warms up, the pieces fall off.)

• Candles

• Plants

Style of worship area and altar size: Any. This altar will work very well in a small space. It is very effective for a contemporary service and can also work well in a retreat setting. The example shown here is designed on a five-and-one-half-foot altar.

Other ideas: For special services, we have given the pieces of broken pottery to participants with a permanent marker. They then write prayers, concerns, or something they wish to give to God on the pottery. Each individual then glues that shard onto the cross. This is a simple device that carries a lot of impact and always receives comment.

Maundy Thursday or Good Friday

Season of use: The Thursday and Friday preceding Easter (the night of the Last Supper and the day of the crucifixion of Christ).

Scripture Reference: Luke 22:10-20 (The account of the Last Supper for use on Maundy Thursday.); Luke 23:44-46 (The account of Jesus' death for use on Good Friday.)

Theme or special focus of the service: Betrayal and crucifixion of Christ, the story of what happened between the triumph of Palm Sunday and joy of the Resurrection

Design concept: Serious, dark, and foreboding. One uses an enlarged old-fashioned picture of Christ on the cross, such as one that might be found in an old illustrated King James Bible. The other incorporates an old piece of needlework found at a flea market.

Number of team members needed to assemble altar: One or two

Supplies needed:
- Fabric
- Candles
- Plants
- Artwork (Please note: If you plan to reproduce artwork, per the 1998 Digital Millennium Copyright Act, permission to copy art for the purpose of one-time display or projection in a worship service or educational setting is generally not needed. However, permission is required if you reproduce the image and hand it out to worshipers.)

Style of worship area and altar size: Any. Works well in more formal spaces and small areas. This could also be used in a fellowship hall or gathering area for soup suppers and special Lenten programs. The example with the larger, horizontal piece of reprographic art is designed on an eleven-foot altar. The other altar table is five-and-one-half-feet long and uses the needlework picture.

Other ideas: On the DVD, you will notice a similar approach with a different piece of needlework.

Spell it Out

Season of use: Any

Suggested Scripture reference: John 11:20–27 (the story of the miracle of the resurrection of Lazarus)

Theme or special focus of the service: A series on the miracles of Christ

Design concept: The Scripture is the main focus. The whole passage is reproduced by a local sign company on an altar cloth, or you might use thin rolled vinyl on which you adhere the letters and then place a solid fabric underneath. (The example shows the latter approach.) This design concept could be used with any passage and any theme.

Number of team members needed to assemble altar: One or two

Supplies needed:
- 54" rolled vinyl (This is available in fabric stores. We chose the "cloudy" or opaque version of vinyl. The clear vinyl was too shiny and would reflect too much for the camera lens.)
- Stick-on lettering
- Green hanging-basket lining (In this example, the lining is what covers the cross.)
- Fabric
- Flowers
- Candle

Style of worship area and altar size: Any, but well suited to contemporary areas and to auditorium-style facilities. This example is designed on an eleven-foot altar.

Other ideas: Measure out the exact area in which the wording will appear. Decide how you want the verses on the plastic. (For instance, we chose not to include the verse numbers and used a font that was easy to read.) Re-roll the plastic after use. Make sure it is stored smooth and without wrinkles. We suggest putting wax paper over the letters, so they don't stick together.

This approach could also be used with high impact in a youth or children's department.

No Dessert Sunday
(What to do when you do not know what to do)

Season of use: Any

Suggested Scripture reference: Any

Theme or special focus of the service: Think of a meal that is so good that you do not need a dessert. This is our philosophy when it comes to the "No Dessert Sunday" design. This phrase has become part of our special altar-design vocabulary. Sometimes it is because there is no visual reference in the Scripture or in the music or special story told by the minister.

Sometimes, it is a seasonal "just because they were blooming today" kind of altar. We never know how and why a particular flower, plant, or texture will affect someone in the congregation. But we guarantee that whatever is used on a timely basis is a gift from God—perhaps something that bloomed specially for that altar.

Design concept: Let your mind flow with what God provides.

Number of team members needed to assemble altar: One or two

Supplies needed: You won't know until you get ready to do your special altar. One of our most awesome altars was filled with large lavender blossoms on tree branches. These came to our altar courtesy of the parking lot of a nearby tire store (and the generosity of the store) and were gathered by standing on top of a pickup truck. Who could have planned something so wonderful? Surely only our Creator God.

Style of worship area and altar size: Absolutely any. This uses the space and style you have available. This example is designed on an eleven-foot altar.

Other ideas: As often as possible, the altar design should intersect with the message and music. However, at certain special times, an idea with outstanding visuals will come to you. Use these sparingly, but do not be afraid to enjoy a gift from God.

Worksheet: Building Upon Ideas

1. What sermon series or special seasons are coming up in our church?

2. Could we adapt one of the sample altars for use in our worship area? How might it differ?

3. Is there someone in our congregation who might build a special cross for us to use on the altar?

To pray about: That the right people will come forward to serve in this ministry, using their special gifts to help others in the worship of God.

Notes:

CHAPTER TEN
Resources to Help Your Efforts

Do not be anxious about anything, but in
    every situation, by prayer and petition,
with thanksgiving, present your requests to
    God.
And the peace of God, which transcends all
    understanding,
will guard your hearts and your minds in
    Christ Jesus.
                 Philippians 4:6-7 (TNIV)

One of our favorite stories about where altar designers find the resources they need comes from a faithful leader at a church in a nearby town. Her story involves a new appreciation for a different kind of altar material: weeds.

Her altar team had traveled to Central Louisiana for a presentation to a group of ten churches in that area. Mary pulled a trailer loaded with supplies behind her van to provide the materials needed to help the groups design the altars. Upon arrival, they set up a variety of sample altars, each connected to specific Scriptures. As the designer says:

We did fine, except when we got to the Communion altar. The visuals consisted of a three-foot vine container, three long loaves of bread, and stalks of wheat. We thought, 'This is easy!' We proceeded to arrange our visuals, and, lo and behold, we didn't have enough to fill the container. What do we do? We are in a strange area; we don't know where to get any fillers, but Mary came to our rescue. She had noticed some Johnson grass in the ditch as we drove to our destination, so off we go with our cutters, gathering Johnson grass by the armload. As we added the Johnson grass to the container, it actually added color and character to the arrangement. Since that day, I have not thought of Johnson grass—something that nobody wants in his or her yard, but can be used in a meaningful and beautiful way—in the same way.

Finding the materials you need for imaginative altars can be a bit like putting a puzzle together. There is no central location where you will find the special items you want or need. Sometimes, starting from scratch, you might begin to feel overwhelmed. When that happens, stop and reflect upon the verses at the beginning of this chapter; do not get anxious about the altar design, but instead ask God for help. Remember the story of the useful weeds and how God guides—sometimes in very unexpected ways.

The work you are doing is for God, not for you, and it will be used accordingly. God has all the answers. Remember the words of an altar designer we met along the way: *"The things you need will be provided by asking."*

Lessons we've learned in finding great sources for altar supplies

- You will not be able to find all that you need from one source. While we can offer you guidelines for finding materials and using them, you will need to use the trial-and-error method as the altar ministry unfolds. Remember, God will give you a better plan than you can ever see in a book. Mary regularly tells how much she enjoys shopping with the Holy Spirit. Sometimes she becomes a power shopper with ideas coming so fast that she has to start jotting them down in the store. She tells her students: "Expect and know this will happen to you—just be ready."

- When you find something that seems perfect for an altar, go ahead and get it, even if you do not know exactly when you will use it. This might seem like an odd way to trust the Holy Spirit, but when you do, you will be amazed.

- Go to out-of-the-way places to look for items. Art shows, craft shows, and trade shows that you thought would never have anything interesting often have useful items. (We once found a great paint color at a boat show!)

- When you make a purchase, let the seller know your intentions for the item. People are fascinated by what we do with the things we buy, and it opens a door to tell people about your church. Folks *love* finding out that a church is using their objects *on the altar!* They tell other customers about it all day, and you will be surprised how many people show up for services to see if you actually used their item.

- Denominations often have their own inventory of altar items. For example, at Cokesbury.com you will find a variety of worship-related items. These include vestments, paraments, and other altar items.

- In chapter 4, we mentioned Cari Bennett Bollinger, an artist on our Creative Ministries Team. She creates stunning visual designs for worship. These are original, thematic paintings on paper or canvas (up to 12′ x 16′). For more information or for samples of her work, e-mail her at cbollinger@sport.rr.com.

Your Altar-Design Budget

- You may find as you start a tribe of altar designers that you have no budget and must pay for items personally. That can be hard, but the blessings you will receive are amazing. We know from experience! As you buy items for the altar, it is important to keep finances in mind and to consider how much use you can get from the items. Reusing items is helpful not only on the altar but also in different areas of your church. We have found that many of our props wind up in special displays in the youth area or in the gathering area in front of the church. In addition, we regularly display artwork and other visual items in the hallways.

- If you receive a budget from your church, you must decide how the money will be allocated. After we created altars the first year, our church gave us a small budget. The second year we decided to spend our budget each year in "chunks" in order to build up an inventory of items frequently needed. We began with "the year of the fabric," followed by "the year of the candlestick," and so on. One year we spent most of our money on metal candle molds, but they last for years, and we now recycle all of our candles.

Search for bargains

Look for other people's cast-offs and special items that are inexpensive. "Start collecting 'stuff,'" says one designer. "Look for items at garage sales or in clearance bins to fit within your budget. When you get that nudge that says you might need that someday, listen to it and have it, because there will come a time when it is just the right item to use for an altar." Another altar team member tells this story:

> My favorite altar story was a Palm Sunday altar. I noticed that a neighbor had trimmed some items and had piled them by the street. When I got closer, I noticed a stack of very large palm branches. That evening as I came home, they were still there, and I couldn't get it out of my head that that sure would be cool for the altar. So, the next morning, armed with gloves (and, out of embarrassment, making sure that nobody was watching), I gingerly put the palm branches in the back of my car. We did not, in fact, have anything for the altar that weekend. It was a tremendous blessing for me to see how they were used. I was definitely glad that I had listened to that "nudge" that said I needed the "trash" from my neighbor's yard.

As you go about your day-to-day shopping, develop an eye for items that can be transformed into the sacred, and purchase them at a discount or on sale whenever possible. Consider these shopping approaches:

- Seek out junk shops and thrift stores.

- Ask friends and family to spread the word that your altar tribe needs "stuff" to use on the altar. Make a list of items you need, and put it in the church bulletin or on the bulletin board. Remember, take whatever shows up! (We once received a dead plant that we smiled and took.)

- Become a regular shopper at discount "dollar" stores or salvage stores. You never know what they might have.

- When you are in your favorite local department store or any store with decorating items, look around to see what designs appear "sacred" to you—candlesticks, pedestals, special crosses, or containers?

- Go to areas of stores where you have never been before. A recent altar project took Mary to the plumbing department at a home improvement store for different sizes of PVC pipe.

- A good collection of fabric is helpful for your design work. Shop sale tables for your basic needs. Every time you go to a discount department store, wheel your buggy over to the discount fabric table. If you see a beautiful piece of fabric that is expensive, know exactly how much you can get by with and buy only that amount. (Keep altar measurements with you at all times.)

The wholesale option

- Buy wholesale whenever possible. This may take some extra planning to get started but can pay off immensely as your altar-design ministry grows. Tag along with those in your congregation who buy at a national wholesale market. Order when possible from the same vendors those people use, and add what you need for the church onto their order. When the order arrives, you are responsible for your share, plus freight. Many times items are backordered, and you may not receive them right away.

- Many vendors have reasonable minimums ($200 or so). Ask vendors, "What is included in your line?" See if there is anything else you can use from that same line to meet the minimum.

- *If you cannot meet the minimum,* take the telephone number of the manufacturer and call it directly. Ask to speak to the owner or to someone in management. Tell them what church you are with and what item you would like to purchase. Ask if they would consider selling that single item to you for use on the altar. Offer to pay a surcharge for their hassle of sending out an individual order.

- If you go with someone to market, there is generally a cost for a "guest pass," but it is well worth it. If you can't afford to buy an item at that time, make notes. When you can, order it. (Don't forget to budget the shipping charges.)

- While at market, soak up the use of colors and textures, and constantly ask yourself, "How could I use that in our church?"

Companies that have been helpful along the way

Businesses come and go, so it is risky to list specific companies from which you might find materials. However, we include these to help you get started. We have done business with most of these companies for years and know them to be helpful and honest. You will see samples of some of their wares on the DVD and in the altar examples in chapter 9.

- **Creative Candles.** This company has taken the ordinary and made it extraordinary. They have unusual lengths of tall tapers (e.g., thirty inches), and the quality is outstanding. We have used their tall candles in our advent wreath for years. They also have all sorts of neat shapes for candles. They usually sell only to the trade but are willing to sell to individual churches.
  PO Box 412514
  Kansas City, MO 64141
  800-237-9711
  E-mail: mail@creativecandles.com
  www.creativecandles.com

- **Burning Butterfly Candles.** This business offers unusual colors, combinations of colors, and textures. They are a little more expensive but well worth it. They will sell to church groups. Their candles have very pleasing light scents.
  1616 Manhattan Ave.
  Union City, NJ 07087
  888-343-2222
  E-mail: customerservice@burningbutterfly.com
  www.burningbutterfly.com (Click on the wholesale information link.)

- **True Vine Wholesale Nursery** is one example of a wholesale nursery that offers trees and shrubs to churches. Located in rural Northwest Louisiana, they have provided many items for our altar and will deliver, depending on the order size and distance. You might find a similar wholesale nursery that is willing to work with churches in your area.
  318-872-0598 or 318-471-4279
  E-mail: truevinenursery@juno.com

  Churches in Tennessee, Kentucky, northern Alabama, and northern Georgia can often work with the dozens of wholesale nurseries that grow trees and shrubs on the Cumberland Plateau near McMinnville, Tennessee.

- **Loose Ends.** These folks are very creative marketers with a great eye for merchandise. They have three catalogues filled to the brim with great fabric, textures, and props. The catalogues cost approximately $10 each, but consider buying them. You will find yourself looking at each page carefully and reading about every item. (This reminds us of the old Sears Wish Book when we were kids.) You can also go online to look at their merchandise, but it is not nearly as much fun as the catalogues. Their curtain panels with shells sewn all over them are the perfect size for an altar covering. Their hand-painted papers are also great for altar design.

  2605 Madrona Ave. SE
  Salem, OR 97302
  503-390-2348
  E-mail: info@looseends.com

- **Stumps.** This is a prom and special-event supplier. (It offers everything you ever need to decorate a gym.) Sign up to receive their catalogue, and look through it carefully. They sell some neat items, such as gossamer, that are inexpensive and work well for altars.
  Stumps Party
  One Party Place
  Box 305
  South Whitley, IN 46787
  800-348-5084
  www.StumpsProm.com or www.StumpsParty.com

- **Rose Brand.** This is a theatrical supply company that offers staging, professional lighting, and nifty stuff that you never before knew existed. We have used their seamless lightweight canvas for whole cloth altars. (This fabric dyes great, takes paint, etc.) They sell really wide cloth (twenty to forty feet wide) with no seams that is great for permanent backdrops and large hangings.
  Rose Brand East
  75 Ninth Ave.
  New York, NY 10011
  800-223-1624
  E-mail: sales@rosebrand.com
  www.rosebrand.com
  or, Rose Brand West
  10616 Lanark St.
  Sun Valley, CA 91352
  800-360-5056

- **Oracle Fountains.** The company is constantly coming up with new fountain ideas. Most of their fountains are very lightweight, made for inside or outside use, and hold up to being dragged in and out of the sanctuary. (The large gray fountain seen on the DVD was ordered from this supplier.)
  Ecosphere Associates, Inc.
  4421 N. Romero Rd.
  Tucson, AZ 85705
  800-729-9870
  E-mail: sales@oraclefountains.com
  www.oraclefountains.com

- **The Lucky Clover Trading Company.** This is a good source for interesting containers, screens, and textures. Their inventory constantly changes.
  4950 E. 2nd St.
  Benicia, CA 94510
  707-746-5885
  www.luckyclovertrading.com

- **Heritage Fire Stones (AKA Oil burning rocks).** Their oil rocks are fantastic for the altar, and people in the congregation always want to know where to get them. We have put them in a youth auction fund-raiser where they were a hot item!
  Park Avenue Candles
  6937 Starpoint Court, Suite C
  Winter Park, FL 32792
  407-671-5588
  www.parkavenuecandles.com

- **Wildwood Specialties.** The owner gathers really cool stuff for people all over the country, including mosses of all types and textures and unusual containers handmade from natural materials. The moss gathered fresh from the mountain areas of Arkansas is incredible. The owner is often in the woods, so be sure to leave a message.
  141 Polk 48
  Mena, AR 71953
  479-394-4987 or 479-394-6059

- **That's Easy.** This business focuses on easy ways to design floral arrangements, and offers glue and miscellaneous hard-to-find design supplies. (It is owned and operated by Mary Dark and Rebecca Seiden.)

3801 Youree Drive
Shreveport, La. 71105
318-219-9935
www.floradot.com

- **BX Glass.** This glass company has unique and high-quality glass containers (stackable and assorted) that work exceptionally well in altar design. Many of their containers make great candleholders. Mention to them that you want to buy wholesale.
    1608 Beach Street
    Montebello, CA 90640
    323-727-8288
    E-mail: sales@bxglassus.com
    www.bxglassus.com

Searching for inspiration

As this wonderful ministry develops, consider resources beyond the items you will purchase for use on the altar. Be open to books and workshops that will help you focus on worship as a whole; this has been crucial in our experiences with the Tribe of Dan ministry in our congregation. Old garden books, such as those put together decades ago by garden clubs, often are full of ideas that can get your creative juices flowing. These can be found in used bookstores and on the Internet (abesbooks.com or allibris.com).

One excellent orientation tool for your altar-design team is *ReConnecting Worship: Where Tradition & Innovation Converge* (Abingdon Press), a small-group study for pastors, worship leaders and planners, and laypersons. Written by Rob Weber and Stacy Hood, this kit (including books and video) explains how experiences such as a vibrant altar ministry can unfold in your congregation. As we have said throughout this book, the Tribe of Dan was born out of a congregation that loves and promotes worship and creativity. The leadership of Pastor Rob and Stacy help make this happen, and they discuss their ideas in detail in *ReConnecting Worship.*

While there are no other books that convey our particular approach to altar design, we recommend four books for inspiration and information. These are: *To Crown the Year—Decorating the Church* by Peter Mazar (Liturgy Training Publications). This is a creative and fun book with great ideas and activities for all ages. *Flowers to the Glory of God* by Sandra S. Hynson (Felfoot Publishers). This book about Washington's National Cathedral has great how-to's, and the illustrations are easy to understand. Many of the ideas are very traditional. *Spaces for Spirit* by Nancy Chinn (Liturgy Training Publications). This is a super, inspiring book about visuals in the church. Although it is not specifically about altars, it helps provoke ideas. *United Methodist Altars: A Guide for the Congregation* by Hoyt L. Hickman (Abingdon Press). This is a basic manual for congregational leaders, explaining how to prepare the sanctuary and its traditional furnishings for the celebration of worship and the sacraments through the Christian year.

Magazines as a source of ideas

Many magazines have ideas that can be adapted for altar use. In addition, florist magazines often can introduce you to new products and manufacturers.

- **Florists' Review**
  PO Box 4368
  Topeka, KS 66604
  800-367-4708
  www.floristsreview.com

- **Flowers& (magazine published by Teleflora)**
  P.O. Box 30130
  Los Angeles, CA 90030-0130
  800-321-2815

- **ARTS (Arts in Religious and Theological Studies)**
  3000 Fifth Street NW
  New Brighton, MN 55112
  651-962-5337
  www.ARTSmag.org

Tribe of Dan and New Wine Design Web sites

TribeofDan.com and NewWineDesign.com can provide you a boost with supply sources. Both of these sites are regularly updated and will provide ideas to help you with your design. In addition, we will continue to add sources to the list above as we discover them.

Mary offers classes in altar design for individuals and groups, does church altar and floral design consultation, and teaches people how to shop at market on trips to the Dallas Market Center. She also is happy to answer questions and offer guidance as churches start Tribe of Dan ministries.

Mary Dark
New Wine Design
3801 Youree Drive
Shreveport, LA 71105
318-219-9935
www.newwinedesign.com

We would love to hear from you about any sources you have found or any ideas you have for awesome altars. We get great joy from stories of the Holy Spirit working through altar design. Please let us hear from you!

E-mail us at newwinedesign@aol.com.

Worksheet: Resources

1. What are some possible sources of altar-design items in our area?

2. What is one step I could take in learning more about altar-design resources?

3. What one item might be most useful for ongoing use on our church's altar?

To pray about: God's provision of items that will enhance the altar and help people as they come into God's presence.

Notes:

A Starting Place for Resourcing Worship

For a detailed list of resources with monthly updates, go to www.robweber.org

Music
www.integritymusic.com
www.vmg.com
www.songdiscovery.com
www.worshiptogether.com
www.worshipmusic.com
www.grassrootsmusic.com
www.ntimemusic.com
www.sheetmusicplus.com
www.jwpepper.com
www.cokesbury.com

Developing Musicians
www.vocalcoach.com
www.worshipinteractive.com
www.christianmusician.com
Many of the Web sites in the first section have training materials for musicians also.

Thematic Search Sites
www.worshipconnection.com
www.willowcreek.com
Willow Creek provides one of the most comprehensive drama script libraries available.

Movie Search Sites
www.imdb.com
www.hollywoodjesus.com

Worship Imagery and Video
www.midnightoilproductions.net
www.highwayvideo.com
www.digitaljuice.com
www.harbingeronline.com
www.umcom.org
www.lumicon.org

Resource Magazines
www.tfwm.com
www.worshipleader.org
www.revmagazine.com

Multimedia Equipment
www.shepherdmin.com
www.fowlerinc.com

Audio Equipment
www.music123.com
www.musiciansfriend.com
www.shure.com
www.yamaha.com
www.dpamicrophones.com
www.wengercorp.com

Copyright Licensing Information
www.churchca.com
www.ccli.com
www.copyclear.com
www.mplc.com
www.swank.com

Miscellaneous Sites:
Sally Morgenthaler's Web site
www.sacramentis.com
Leonard Sweet
www.leonardsweet.com
Howard Hanger
www.howardhanger.com
www.jubileecommunity.org